Student Life

Other Books of Related Interest:

Opposing Viewpoints Series

Child Custody

Popular Culture

School Reform

At Issue Series

Are Social Networking Sites Harmful?

Cell Phones and Driving

Should Junk Food Be Sold in Schools?

Current Controversies Series

Teen Preganancy and Parenting

Teens and Privacy

"Congress shall make no law . . . abridging the freedom of speech, or of the press."

First Amendment to the U.S. Constitution

The basic foundation of our democracy is the First Amendment guarantee of freedom of expression. The Opposing Viewpoints Series is dedicated to the concept of this basic freedom and the idea that it is more important to practice it than to enshrine it.

OPPOSING
VIEWPOINTS®
SERIES

Student Life

Karen Miller, Book Editor

GREENHAVEN PRESS
A part of Gale, Cengage Learning

GALE
CENGAGE Learning™

Detroit • New York • San Francisco • New Haven, Conn • Waterville, Maine • London

Christine Nasso, *Publisher*
Elizabeth Des Chenes, *Managing Editor*

© 2011 Greenhaven Press, a part of Gale, Cengage Learning.

For more information, contact:
Greenhaven Press
27500 Drake Rd.
Farmington Hills, MI 48331-3535
Or you can visit our Internet site at http://www.gale.cengage.com

For product information and technology assistance, contact us at

Gale Customer Support, 1-800-877-4253
For permission to use material from this text or product, submit all requests online at
www.cengage.com/permissions

Further permissions questions can be emailed to permissionrequest@cengage.com

Articles in Greenhaven Press anthologies are often edited for length to meet page require-ments. In addition, original titles of these works are changed to clearly present the main thesis and to explicitly indicate the author's opinion. Every effort is made to ensure that Greenhaven Press accurately reflects the original intent of the authors. Every effort has been made to trace the owners of copyrighted material.

Cover Image copyright © Unweit|Dreamstime.com.

LIBRARY OF CONGRESS CATALOGING-IN-PUBLICATION DATA

Student life / Karen Miller, book editor.
    p. cm. -- (Opposing viewpoints)
    Includes bibliographical references and index.
    ISBN 978-0-7377-4990-8 (hardcover) -- ISBN 978-0-7377-4991-5 (pbk.)
    1. Students--Social life and customs--United States. 2. Education--United States.
3. Attitude (Psychology) I. Miller, Karen.
    LA216.S783 2011
    378.1'98--dc22
                                                        2010037591

Printed in the United States of America
1 2 3 4 5 6 7 14 13 12 11 10

Contents

Chapter 3: Do Campus Athletic Programs Benefit Students?

Chapter 4: What Issues Do Greek Letter Organizations Face?

Why Consider Opposing Viewpoints?

> "The only way in which a human being can make some approach to knowing the whole of a subject is by hearing what can be said about it by persons of every variety of opinion and studying all modes in which it can be looked at by every character of mind. No wise man ever acquired his wisdom in any mode but this."
>
> *John Stuart Mill*

In our media-intensive culture it is not difficult to find differing opinions. Thousands of newspapers and magazines and dozens of radio and television talk shows resound with differing points of view. The difficulty lies in deciding which opinion to agree with and which "experts" seem the most credible. The more inundated we become with differing opinions and claims, the more essential it is to hone critical reading and thinking skills to evaluate these ideas. Opposing Viewpoints books address this problem directly by presenting stimulating debates that can be used to enhance and teach these skills. The varied opinions contained in each book examine many different aspects of a single issue. While examining these conveniently edited opposing views, readers can develop critical thinking skills such as the ability to compare and contrast authors' credibility, facts, argumentation styles, use of persuasive techniques, and other stylistic tools. In short, the Opposing Viewpoints Series is an ideal way to attain the higher-level thinking and reading skills so essential in a culture of diverse and contradictory opinions.

In addition to providing a tool for critical thinking, Opposing Viewpoints books challenge readers to question their own strongly held opinions and assumptions. Most people form their opinions on the basis of upbringing, peer pressure, and personal, cultural, or professional bias. By reading carefully balanced opposing views, readers must directly confront new ideas as well as the opinions of those with whom they disagree. This is not to argue simplistically that everyone who reads opposing views will—or should—change his or her opinion. Instead, the series enhances readers' understanding of their own views by encouraging confrontation with opposing ideas. Careful examination of others' views can lead to the readers' understanding of the logical inconsistencies in their own opinions, perspective on why they hold an opinion, and the consideration of the possibility that their opinion requires further evaluation.

Evaluating Other Opinions

To ensure that this type of examination occurs, Opposing Viewpoints books present all types of opinions. Prominent spokespeople on different sides of each issue as well as well-known professionals from many disciplines challenge the reader. An additional goal of the series is to provide a forum for other, less known, or even unpopular viewpoints. The opinion of an ordinary person who has had to make the decision to cut off life support from a terminally ill relative, for example, may be just as valuable and provide just as much insight as a medical ethicist's professional opinion. The editors have two additional purposes in including these less known views. One, the editors encourage readers to respect others' opinions—even when not enhanced by professional credibility. It is only by reading or listening to and objectively evaluating others' ideas that one can determine whether they are worthy of consideration. Two, the inclusion of such viewpoints encourages the important critical thinking skill of objectively evaluating an author's credentials and bias. This evaluation will illuminate an author's reasons for taking a particular stance on an issue and will aid in readers' evaluation of the author's ideas.

It is our hope that these books will give readers a deeper understanding of the issues debated and an appreciation of the complexity of even seemingly simple issues when good and honest people disagree. This awareness is particularly important in a democratic society such as ours in which people enter into public debate to determine the common good. Those with whom one disagrees should not be regarded as enemies but rather as people whose views deserve careful examination and may shed light on one's own.

Thomas Jefferson once said that "difference of opinion leads to inquiry, and inquiry to truth." Jefferson, a broadly educated man, argued that "if a nation expects to be ignorant and free . . . it expects what never was and never will be." As individuals and as a nation, it is imperative that we consider the opinions of others and examine them with skill and discernment. The Opposing Viewpoints Series is intended to help readers achieve this goal.

David L. Bender and Bruno Leone,
Founders

Introduction

> *"The power of a father, I say, over the persons of his children ceases at the age of twenty-one. . . . Yet, till that age arrives, . . . he may also delegate part of his parental authority, during his life, to the tutor or schoolmaster of his child; who is then in* loco parentis, *and has such a portion of the power of the parent committed to his charge, viz. that of restraint and correction, as may be necessary to answer the purposes for which he is employed."*
>
> —Sir William Blackstone,
> Commentaries on the
> Laws of England, Book 1:
> The Rights of Persons, *1765–1769*

The age at which a minor child becomes an adult is not universally agreed upon, by either politicians and biologists or parents and their offspring. Adult privileges and responsibilities are doled out gradually, beginning for many in early adolescence. While the age of majority throughout most of the United States is eighteen, state and federal laws grant certain rights to young people at various ages. In some states, teenagers are legally able to marry without parental permission before they are old enough to get a tattoo; throughout the United States, young people can join the military and vote years before they are legally allowed to buy alcohol. No clear boundary between childhood and adulthood exists, but for many, the transition between the two states takes place largely during undergraduate years. This circumstance places parents, university personnel, and college students into murky territory in terms of their relationships with and responsibilities to each other.

In loco parentis is a Latin term that means "in the place of a parent." When parents send a twelve-year-old to a sleepaway summer camp, they entrust camp directors and counselors with the parental responsibility of maintaining the health and protecting the morals of that child. When parents send eighteen-year-olds to live at college, they expect similar services from professors and staff. Universities have student judicial boards, mental health and academic counselors, activities directors, and even official resident advisors who live among students on campus to make sure that they follow rules and get personal help when they need it.

Since their founding, universities have closely monitored the moral and physical well-being of students on behalf of their guardians; a school is referred to as an *alma mater*—a "nourishing mother"—for a reason. In the Middle Ages, Merton College (now part of the University of Oxford) attempted to stifle gossip by allowing students to converse only in Latin and forbidding them from meeting in their rooms to talk for any reason. In 1800, in what is today Princeton University, three students who disrupted morning prayers by scraping their boots against the wooden floor were expelled. Rules regarding dormitory visitors endured well into the second half of the twentieth century, and some campuses still maintain bans on members of the opposite sex in rooms. Some religious schools require students to forswear dancing—on campus and off—and enforce dress codes. Many universities have students sign statements of academic integrity and promise not to cheat or plagiarize. Such policies are established to compel students to behave the way a university believes they should behave—to turn them into upstanding, admirable representatives of its traditions and ideals.

Most college students, however, are old enough to be legal adults and are guaranteed certain rights that accompany coming of age. Regardless of who pays the tuition, the person receiving the diploma is the primary client, and a student who thinks that a university tasked with expanding his or her intellect meddles too much in personal decisions will move off campus or transfer to another school. Furthermore, the "college experience" of learning to live independently looms in the cultural consciousness as a type of training for adulthood that many consider as important as learning how to write or become an engineer. It takes a lot of practice to learn how to be a responsible adult, and students who never learn how to manage their schedules and cope with relationship conflicts are not likely to navigate the social and political environment of a professional workplace. Schools that step too much into a parent's shoes might impede such personal growth, hindering rather than helping their students.

Striking a balance between nurturing and corralling students, between nudging them toward accepting increasing amounts of personal responsibility and restricting their behavior, is an ongoing process for educational institutions just as it is for parents. The 1974 Family Educational Rights and Privacy Act (FERPA) was passed to ensure that information about a student's grades, health records, and disciplinary history was officially under the student's control and could be disclosed to other parties (such as parents or employers) only with his or her permission; this law implies that even students receiving financial support are mature enough to take care of their personal business. Co-ed dormitories (and even mixed-sex bathrooms) carry this assumption further and make students responsible for relationships conducted in their living space.

College years are formative years, and where a student goes to school and how he or she interacts with peers and faculty directly influence the kind of adult he or she will become. *Opposing Viewpoints: Student Life* explores how campus institutions and organizations affect student lives and development. Its four chapters, Do College Students Engage in Risky

Behaviors? Do Students Receive Adequate Health Care on Campus? Do Campus Athletic Programs Benefit Students? and What Issues Do Greek Letter Organizations Face? identify some of the factors that color a student's experience and explore the complexities of student life.

CHAPTER 1

Do College Students Engage in Risky Behaviors?

Chapter Preface

"Tanorexia" is an informal term (a combination of "tan" and "anorexia") that refers to the habit some people have of going to the tanning salon too often—as often as one hundred times a year. Although tan skin can be acquired with lotions and makeup, some people insist on using tanning beds despite the increased risks of skin cancer from the ultraviolet (UV) radiation in the light. Frequent clients of tanning salons cite a variety of reasons for visiting so often, some of which indicate psychological disorders. For example, extreme tanners may suffer from a form of body dysmorphic disorder (BDD) and perceive their skin as unacceptably pale no matter how tan they get. More common, however, is the claim that reclining on a tanning bed is their only chance for undisturbed relaxation and that tanning indoors provides stress release.

Researchers Catherine Mosher and Sharon Danoff-Burg published the results of their study about the use of tanning beds among college students from a northeastern school in the April 2010 issue of *Archives of Dermatology*. Of the 429 students surveyed, more than half (229 students) reported tanning indoors, and more than a third of those 229 students met the criteria for addiction on standard psychological screening tests. Seventy-eight percent of these "tanning addicts" confessed that they had tried to stop tanning and couldn't; nearly a quarter admitted they had missed a class or a social function just to go to a tanning salon.

Mandeep Kaur led a team of doctors in a study of how ultraviolet light itself—the spectrum of light that actually tans skin—might contribute to a tanning addiction. The report in the April 2006 issue of the *Journal of the American Academy of Dermatology* argues that UV light triggers the production of endorphins in the brain. Endorphins are neurotransmitters that positively influence mood and cause a person to feel relaxed and enjoy a state of well-being. Long exercise sessions are one way to release endorphins into the brain (think of the phenomenon known as "runner's high"); an indoor tanning session is another. Tanning addicts may first patronize a salon to prepare their skin for a vacation or a formal event, but then return again and again for psychological and chemical benefits. In an April 20, 2010, article in the *Los Angeles Times*, Steven Feldman, senior author of the Kaur study, compared a session in a tanning bed to getting a small narcotic hit. Self-tanning sprays and lotions turn skin the same color, but they provide no more "kick" than applying hand cream. In the end, the tan itself is just a side effect.

Going to college can be a stressful experience, and the long winters in some climates can be depressing. Tanning salons are relatively cheap and within easy reach of campus, and a visit can promise a quiet interlude in a busy day. Students who turn to tanning as a quick pick-me-up rarely intend to become addicted to the experience, but some become dependent on it despite their knowledge of the risks of cancer. What starts as a harmless activity can turn into a disruptive, dangerous habit with long-term, life-threatening consequences. The following chapter examines other risky activities college students engage in and explores the extent to which these behaviors are destructive and their prevalence in campus society.

> *"Reframing college drinking changed the issue from a personal trouble of an individual alcoholic or habitual drunk to a public issue involving an entire population at risk."*

College Drinking Is a Serious Problem

George W. Dowdall

George W. Dowdall is a professor of sociology at St. Joseph's University in Philadelphia; he serves on the Pennsylvania Advisory Council on Drug and Alcohol Abuse. The following viewpoint is excerpted from his book, College Drinking: Reframing a Social Problem, *which explores the ways that the view of college drinking as a carefree rite of passage has changed to the idea that reckless alcohol use and abuse has become embedded in college culture with serious negative personal and social consequences. Dowdall explores the financial costs of binge drinking as well as how binge drinkers hurt themselves and others.*

As you read, consider the following questions:

1. According to Dowdall, what percentage of students surveyed by Harvard University reported binge drinking?

2. What types of problems, according to the author, would be considered "secondhand effects" of binge drinking?

3. In Dowdall's view, what is a likely reason for the large discrepancy between the number of college students who died for alcohol-related reasons that was reported in *USA Today* and the number that was reported by epidemiologist Ralph Hingson?

Many students have adopted a drinking style that centers on frequent or intense alcohol consumption. When . . . Harvard researchers [who conducted college alcohol studies throughout the 1990s] asked about their activities during the month before the survey, a large minority (44 percent) of students told them they binged, and often drank with the intention of getting drunk. Depending on the survey year, between 20 and 33 percent of students said they had been drunk three or more times in the previous month, and a slightly smaller percentage drank on 10 or more days over the course of the month.

Men were somewhat more likely than women to respond positively to these items, though the gap was not great. Over the long term, the changes in women's drinking behaviors have been quite large, but even today the gap remains between the genders.

For some students, drinking is not associated with any immediate negative outcomes. But heavy episodic or binge drinking raises the risk of alcohol-related problems. . . . Bingers are more likely than non-bingers to get behind in schoolwork, get into trouble with campus or community police, have unprotected or unplanned sex, or face other alcohol-related problems. Occasional binge drinkers have a higher risk of these problems than do non-bingeing drinkers, and frequent binge drinkers have the highest risk of all.

There is a strong, positive correlation between the frequency of binge drinking and alcohol-related health and other problems reported by students. With regard to the more serious alcohol-related problems, the frequent binge drinkers were 7 to 10 times more likely than the non-binge drinkers to get into trouble with campus police, damage property or get injured, not use protection when having sex, or engage in unplanned sexual activity. Men and women report similar incidence for most of the problems. Among the frequent binge drinkers, however, 35 percent of the men and 9 percent of the women report damaging property and 16 percent of the men and 6 percent of the women report getting into trouble with the campus police.

There is a positive relationship between binge drinking and driving under the influence of alcohol, and a large proportion of the student population reported driving after drinking alcohol. Binge drinkers reported significantly higher frequencies of dangerous driving behaviors than non-binge drinkers. The 1999 Harvard study reported driving after drinking by one in five non-bingeing students, two in five of the occasional binge drinkers, and almost three in five of the frequent binge drinkers. As many as 2.8 million college students ages 18–24 drove under the influence of alcohol in 2001.

About one-half of the frequent binge drinkers (47 percent in 1993 and 52 percent in 1997) reported having experienced, since the beginning of the school year, five or more of a possible 12 alcohol-related problems (e.g., omitting hangover and including driving after drinking), compared with 14 percent of infrequent binge drinkers and 3 percent of non-binge drinkers. Frequent binge drinkers were 20 (1997) to 25 (1993) times more likely than non-binge drinkers to experience five or more of these problems. . . .

Secondhand Effects

Almost a third of the Harvard study's colleges have a majority of students who binge. These binge drinkers not only put themselves at risk, but also create problems for their non-bingeing fellow students. Non-bingeing students on high-binge campuses were up to three times as likely to report being bothered by the drinking-related behaviors of other students than non-bingeing students at lower-binge campuses. These problems include being pushed, hit or assaulted, and experiencing an unwanted sexual advance.

Secondary or secondhand binge effects—that is, effects on others around the drinker—were examined by the Harvard researchers. They examined the percentage of non-bingeing students who experienced secondary binge effects, which include eight types of problems caused by other students' drinking. . . . These secondary effects range from being insulted or humiliated, to having studying or sleep interrupted, to being a victim of sexual assault. Students at middle- and high-binge-level schools were more likely than students at lower-binge-level schools to experience such secondary problems as a result of the drinking behaviors of others. Specifically, students at the highest-binge-level schools were three times as likely to experience at least one of these eight problems than students at lower-binge-level schools.

Alcohol Dependence and Abuse

Some binge drinkers—and many frequent binge drinkers—appear to match the clinical definitions of having a problem with alcohol, and thus should be receiving treatment. But many of these students deny they have a problem, and haven't sought treatment.

The epidemiologist Deborah Dawson and her colleagues analyzed data from a large national survey, the 2001–02 National Epidemiologic Survey on Alcohol and Related Conditions (NESARC) for adults ages 18–29. The NESARC includes questionnaire items that indicate whether a person meets the criteria for having an alcohol use disorder. College students were found to have slightly higher rates of both [alcohol abuse and alcohol dependence]. The data show that 7.8 percent of all college students (and 10.3 percent of past-year college student drinkers) meet the abuse criteria, while 10.9 percent of all students and 14.5 percent of drinkers meet the dependence criteria. In all, 18.7 percent of all students and 24.7 percent of college drinkers meet the criteria for either alcohol abuse or dependence.

These are not simple findings, however, because it is unclear how the disorders develop, how many precede going to college, and what impact (if any) the college environment has on their progression. But demonstrating this powerful connection between college drinking and serious psychiatric disorder should make it clear that college drinking is not a harmless rite of passage.

Fatalities

Reframing college drinking as a social problem involves illuminating some of the darkest areas of college life, such as student fatalities involving alcohol. The stunning headlines about alcohol-related deaths at institutions across the country make this an issue of intense public interest. However, the enumeration of several dozen deaths each year in newspaper headlines hardly constitutes a definitive assessment of the extent of the problem.

USA Today gathered data on 857 deaths to college students in the years from 2000 to 2005, finally examining 620 deaths involving four-year college students, occurring within or related to the college community or campus, and taking place while classes were in session. The reporters made use of a number of sources to compile these data and noted how difficult it was to gather the information.

By contrast, the epidemiologist Ralph Hingson prepared several estimates of the number of college students of traditional college age (18–24 years) who experience alcohol-related deaths, constituting the best estimate of the most serious outcomes of college drinking. Hingson estimated more than 1,400

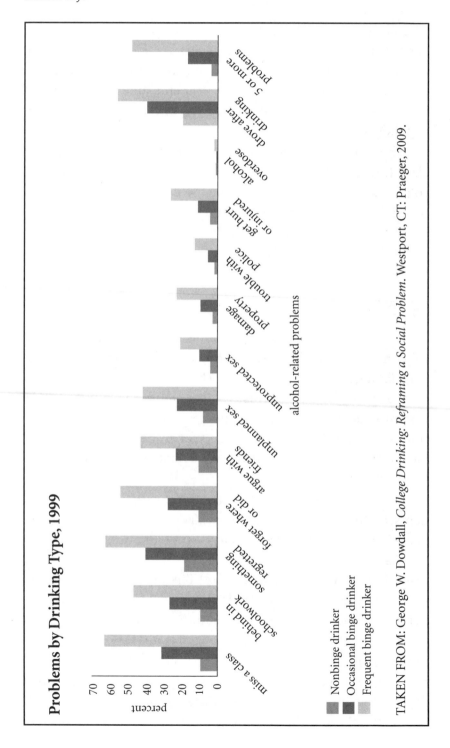

Problems by Drinking Type, 1999

miss a class

behind in schoolwork

something regretted

forget where or did

argue with friends

unplanned sex

unprotected sex

damage property

trouble with police

get hurt or injured

alcohol overdose

drove after drinking

5 or more problems

alcohol-related problems

percent

0 10 20 30 40 50 60 70

Nonbinge drinker

Occasional binge drinker

Frequent binge drinker

TAKEN FROM: George W. Dowdall, *College Drinking: Reframing a Social Problem.* Westport, CT: Praeger, 2009.

student deaths in 1998, and more than 1,700 deaths in 2001, an increase of 6 percent over the period. Many of the deaths, perhaps 80 percent, were due to alcohol-related car crashes, many of which probably occurred off campus and some of which occurred during summer and other vacations.

So, 1,700 alcohol-related deaths in a single year were estimated by Hingson, whereas 620 deaths of any kind were found for five years in the public news and other sources used by *USA Today*. Most college student deaths are probably not reported in the media. This glaring gap in data collection reflects the fact that American death certificates do not routinely report whether the deceased was a college student. Public attention usually focuses on student deaths that occur on campus during the academic year, with less known about deaths under other circumstances.

Alcohol abuse also raises the risk of suicide among young people, and alcohol is involved in two-thirds of college student suicides. The increase in the minimum legal drinking age during the 1980s is estimated to have saved 125 lives from suicide per year among youths ages 18 to 20 years.

Hard and Soft Costs

From the facts above, it is obvious that the costs of college binge drinking must be substantial, but no precise estimates exist. Estimates are available, however, of the related problem of the costs of underage drinking. Note that underage drinking includes a far larger population than college binge drinking: the large number of Americans of traditional college age who don't go to college as well as those of high school age or younger are included in the former but not the latter.

Far from being trivial, the annual overall cost of alcohol use by those under 21 was estimated at more than $58 billion dollars in 1999. One estimate, prepared for the U.S. Department of Justice, Office of Juvenile Justice and Delinquency

Prevention, used current health and criminal justice data to arrive at these broad components:

- Violent crime: $35 billion

- Traffic crashes: $18 billion

- Suicide attempts: $1.5 billion

- Treatment: $1 billion

- Drowning: $0.5 billion

- Fetal alcohol syndrome: $0.5 billion

- Burns: $0.3 billion

- Alcohol poisonings: $0.3 billion

What colleges end up paying for college drinking is difficult, perhaps impossible, to estimate. Dividing the costs into hard (actual dollars) and soft (loss of reputation, institutional focus) helps us to begin an accounting for the entire bill. Many of the hard costs find their way into charges for room and board for residential students, and into student affairs and public safety costs passed on in higher tuition bills for all students. Some fraction of community police and public safety costs in communities with college campuses also go to covering the costs of college drinking. As for the soft costs, those are even harder to estimate: Some part of the reputation and public regard that higher education has developed must be affected by the negative view of college drinking, although to some this view may make college more attractive. On the other hand, the local alcohol outlets and the industry that supports them sell a significant amount of product to students both of and below legal age.

Snapshot of Health Consequences

The evidence reviewed so far shows that heavy episodic or binge drinking is associated with a much higher risk of negative health and behavioral outcomes. To bring home how many students are actually affected by college drinking, Ralph Hingson and his colleagues used these and similar data to make estimates of the magnitude of alcohol-related morbidity (illness) and mortality (death) among college students of traditional college age (18–24), producing the following "snapshot":

> The consequences of excessive and underage drinking affect virtually all college campuses, college communities, and college students, whether they choose to drink or not.
>
> - *Death*: 1,700 college students between the ages of 18 and 24 die each year from alcohol-related unintentional injuries, including motor vehicle crashes.
>
> - *Injury*: 599,000 students between the ages of 18 and 24 are unintentionally injured under the influence of alcohol.
>
> - *Assault*: More than 696,000 students between the ages of 18 and 24 are assaulted by another student who has been drinking.
>
> - *Sexual Abuse*: More than 97,000 students between the ages of 18 and 24 are victims of alcohol-related sexual assault or date rape.
>
> - *Unsafe Sex*: 400,000 students between the ages of 18 and 24 had unprotected sex and more than 100,000 students between the ages of 18 and 24 report having been too intoxicated to know if they consented to having sex.
>
> - *Academic Problems*: About 25 percent of college students report academic consequences of their drinking including missing class, falling behind, doing poorly on exams or papers, and receiving lower grades overall.
>
> - *Health Problems/Suicide Attempts*: More than 150,000 students develop an alcohol-related health problem . . .

29

and between 1.2 and 1.5 percent of students indicate that they tried to commit suicide within the past year due to drinking or drug use.

- *Drunk Driving*: 2.1 million students between the ages of 18 and 24 drove under the influence of alcohol last year.

- *Vandalism*: About 11 percent of college student drinkers report that they have damaged property while under the influence of alcohol.

- *Property Damage*: More than 25 percent of administrators from schools with relatively low drinking levels and over 50 percent from schools with high drinking levels say their campuses have a "moderate" or "major" problem with alcohol-related property damage.

- *Police Involvement*: About 5 percent of four-year college students are involved with the police or campus security as a result of their drinking . . . and an estimated 110,000 students between the ages of 18 and 24 are arrested for an alcohol-related violation such as public drunkenness or driving under the influence.

- *Alcohol Abuse and Dependence*: 31 percent of college students met criteria for a diagnosis of alcohol abuse and 6 percent for a diagnosis of alcohol dependence in the past 12 months, according to questionnaire-based self-reports about their drinking.

This snapshot may well be an underestimate of the current health and behavioral consequences of college drinking. It does not take into account such issues as suicide. Nor does it attempt to deal with the problems of mixing alcohol with other substances, such as prescription drugs, thought to be on the rise among young populations. It points to academic problems, but it does not attempt to estimate the impact alcohol abuse might have on not completing college. . . .

Reframing college drinking changed the issue from a personal trouble of an individual alcoholic or habitual drunk to a public issue involving an entire population at risk. Reframing also shifted the focus from harmless though perhaps embarrassing consequences for the individual drinker to serious and even deadly consequences for both the drinker and those in the immediate environment.

| "The Youth Risk Behavior Surveillance survey ... has demonstrated decreases in various measures of alcohol use in the last 10 to 15 years."

College Alcohol Use Is on the Decline

Erin M. English, Michael D. Shutt, and Sara B. Oswalt

Erin M. English is the Alcohol and Other Drug Prevention coordinator at the University of Georgia; Michael D. Shutt is the assistant dean for Campus Life at Emory University; Sara B. Oswalt is an assistant professor in the Department of Health and Kinesiology at the University of Texas at San Antonio. In the following viewpoint, they analyze statistics about youth alcohol use from a five-year study of incoming freshmen at a large, public university in the southeastern United States. They assess the study results in the context of the personality characteristics of the "Millennial" generation, the group of people born between 1982 and 2000 (some of whom attend college now). The authors argue that Millennials' preference for low-risk, less rebellious behaviors has lead to decreasing alcohol consumption rates overall. They note an increase in racial and ethnic diversity at this

Erin M. English, Michael D. Shutt, and Sara B. Oswalt, "Decreasing Use of Alcohol, Tobacco, and Other Drugs on a College Campus: Exploring Potential Factors Related to Change," *Journal of Student Affairs Research and Practice*, vol. 46, 2009, pp. 163–182.

school, pointing out that an increase in campus diversity predicts lower alcohol use. The authors conclude that the findings of studies on alcohol-related problems should inform prevention programs at universities.

As you read, consider the following questions:

1. According to the authors, what are the most common lifetime goals of people in the Millennial generation?
2. How has school-age alcohol use changed in the years from 1991 to 2007, as presented by the authors?
3. What is the relationship, reported by the authors, between college campus ethnic diversity and binge alcohol drinking rates?

One limitation of current [alcohol] prevention efforts is a lack of consideration for how the college student population may be changing. The Youth Risk Behavior Surveillance survey, a national representative survey for ninth- through twelfth-grade students, has demonstrated decreases in various measures of alcohol use in the last 10 to 15 years. In order to create change on college campuses in regard to student ATOD [alcohol, tobacco, and other drugs] use behaviors, campus administrators should consider the unique characteristics of incoming students, as well as the interactions among these characteristics, health behaviors, and the campus environment.

The Millennial generation, those born between 1982 and 2000, began entering college in 2000. An understanding of how this group of students is different, academically, socially, and developmentally than previous generations is important for being proactive—instead of reactive—in providing effective substance abuse prevention services. Characteristics that define the Millennial generation include a need for structure, respect for authority, comfort with parental values, desire for achievement, and a tendency to follow rules. Many of these characteristics derive from a childhood experience emphasizing the uniqueness of the individual, highlighting the concept of no winners or losers, and providing a supportive environment with extremely involved parents. Manifestations of some of these characteristics can be found in a [2007 Pew Research Center] report that focused on a subset of the Millennial generation, specifically, those born before 1988. For example, 80% of those surveyed reported talking to their parents in the past day with nearly 75% seeing their parents at least once a week, and half seeing their parents daily. The majority of these participants (64%) identified family—and primarily mothers—as the individuals from whom they sought advice regarding personal issues. Likewise, the most common goals that individuals of this generation specifically identified for their group were financial success and fame. This subgroup also has a positive outlook on the federal government.

This Millennial generation is also ethnically and culturally diverse—20% have an immigrant parent and 10% have a parent who is not a U.S. citizen. And most of this generation (70% according to [William] Strauss & [Neil] Howe [in *Millennials Go to College*]) plans to attend college. The Pew report shows a similar interest in higher education: Of those who are currently in school, 81% plan to obtain at least a bachelor's degree; and of those who are not in school, 68% plan to return to school in the future.

Exploring Current Trends

Given these factors in addition to data from the Youth Risk Behavior Surveillance survey, this generation of students may be bringing a very different set of behaviors to college campuses. Rather than creating a college experience rife with rebellion and high-risk behaviors, the Millennial generation may set a new, low-risk tone on campuses. Because prevention efforts have yielded minimal results over the last two decades, campuses should examine student demographics and generational characteristics in conjunction with ATOD prevalence data to more productively inform prevention education initiatives. In order to better understand the current incoming college student population and its unique needs, this study sought to answer the following research questions:

- What are the trends in current ATOD use among incoming first-time, first-year college students?

- What are the trends in the intent to use ATOD in college among incoming first-time, first-year college students?

- What are the demographic trends in ATOD use among incoming first-time, first-year college students? ...

Surveying Classes of College Freshmen

Questions on the survey addressed two areas: (a) the incoming students' current use of substances (i.e., alcohol, tobacco, marijuana, and other illegal drug use), and (b) their intent to use alcohol during their first year of college. There were five questions regarding current use. Four questions asked about use of alcohol, tobacco, marijuana, and other illegal drugs in the last year with possible responses including did not use, once a year, six times a year, once a month, twice a month, once a week, three times a week, five times a week, and every day. For these four items, the specific question read, "Within the last year, about how often have you used (insert substance)?" One question asked the incoming students to reflect on the last time they "partied"/socialized and provide how many drinks they had; specifically the question read, "The last time you partied/socialized, how many alcoholic drinks did you have?" No definition for partying/socializing was given. These questions were open-ended, and the students wrote in a response.

Two questions asked about the incoming students' intent to use alcohol during the first year of college. One item included possible responses of: do not plan to use, once a year, six times a year, once a month, twice a month, once a week, three times a week, five times a week, and every day. The other item asked for the average number of drinks they plan to consume each occasion they drink during their first year of college. The last three questions asked for demographic information (i.e., gender, ethnicity) and whether students planned to join a fraternity or sorority. . . .

Examination of the incoming students' intentions to use alcohol revealed significant differences regarding frequency of intended drinking, with more incoming students in 2006 intending to not drink at all while in college (44.0%) compared to previous years. . . . There were also significant differences between all three response categories [yes, no, maybe] for the decision to join a fraternity. . . . Regarding significant differences among ethnicities, black respondents reported a fewer number of intended drinks than all other groups except Asian respondents. . . . There was also a significant difference between white and Asian participants with Asian respondents reporting a lower intended number of drinks . . . than white respondents.

Analyzing the Results

Significant differences existed between the years regarding current ATOD use and intended alcohol use by incoming students. These differences echo changes in alcohol use of school-age youth as measured by the Youth Risk Behavior Surveillance survey. The national representative survey demonstrates decreases in lifetime alcohol use from 1991 to 2007, decreases in current alcohol use from 1999 to 2007, and decreases in high-risk drinking in the last 30 days from 1997 to 2007 in ninth-through twelfth-grade students. The lower alcohol and other drug use demonstrated in the Youth Risk Behavior Surveillance study and the results of the current study are consistent with the Millennial generation's tendency to follow rules and to be risk averse.

Intended Alcohol Use of Incoming First-Time First-Year Students

	2002		2004		2006	
	Percentage	Number	Percentage	Number	Percentage	Number
Never	34.1%	623	38.1%	903	44.0%	776
Once a year	2.6%	47	3.4%	81	2.8%	50
6 times a year	5.3%	98	6.9%	163	7.2%	128
Once a month	9.1%	166	9.2%	219	10.5%	186
Twice a month	11.9%	218	11.8%	280	11.8%	208
Once a week	21.9%	400	19.4%	461	18.0%	318
3 times a week	12.7%	231	9.3%	221	5.2%	91
5 times a week	1.6%	29	1.3%	31	0.2%	3
Every day	0.8%	14	0.6%	14	0.3%	5
Total	100.0%	1,826	100.0%	2,373	100.0%	1,765

TAKEN FROM: Erin M. English, Michael D. Shutt, and Sara B. Oswalt, "Decreasing Use of Alcohol, Tobacco, and other Drugs on a College Campus," *Journal of Student Affairs Research and Practice*, 2009.

The current study's results also demonstrated differences in drinking behaviors based on race and gender for these study participants. Specifically for those incoming students surveyed, the data showed that women drink less and intend to drink less than men and that students of color drink less and intend to drink less than white students, which is consistent with previous research.

This study revealed a change in the demographic makeup among participants over time, which parallels the changing demographics among students at this particular institution and across the nation. From 2002 to 2006 at this university [a large, public university in the southeastern United States], the number of participants identifying as students of color increased. Nationally, the number and proportion of students of color attending college has increased since 1995, but trend data for the last 10 years is not available. These study results demonstrate an increase in racial diversity and concomitant decreases in ATOD use at this institution. This is consistent with the findings by [D.C.] Siebert and colleagues (2003), which demonstrated that ethnic diversity on campus predicts lower alcohol use. In one study, even the binge drinking rates among white, male, and underage students were lower at institutions with more racially/ethnically diverse students, women, and older students. The current study shows ethnicity as a factor affecting number of drinks consumed and number of drinks intended to be consumed, but the interaction of year and ethnicity was not a significant factor. . . . As more students of color from the Millennial generation matriculate to college, the connection to substance use rates needs to be closely examined.

Alcohol Awareness and Prevention Programs for Millennials

One of the major outcomes of the national focus on alcohol-related problems on college campuses is a foundation of research that delineates effective, promising, and ineffective strategies in relation to alcohol abuse prevention. The task force of the National Advisory Council [on Alcohol Abuse and Alcoholism] for the NIAAA [National Institute on Alcohol Abuse and Alcoholism] made several recommendations to combat college drinking in its 2002 study, *A Call to Action: Changing the Culture of Drinking at U.S. Colleges.* These recommended strategies were divided into tiers of effectiveness: tier one strategies demonstrated evidence of effectiveness among college students, tier two strategies demonstrated evidence of success with general populations that could be applied to college environments, tier three strategies provided evidence of logical and theoretical promise, and tier four strategies proved to be ineffective.

It is important to consider these tiers and the individual strategies that will be most successful with the incoming college student of this generation. The tier two strategies that could support the characteristics of the incoming student include environmental factors that discourage high-risk ATOD use, for example, through consistent enforcement of alcohol policies and laws by both campus administrators and community police. Other strategies include reducing alcohol license density, increasing prices and excise taxes on alcoholic beverages, providing responsible beverage service training, and creating effective campus/community coalitions. For the Millennial student, who likes to follow the rules and obey authority, these actions reinforce their beliefs that obeying regulations is important. Moreover, these strategies help to eliminate the "mixed messages" that have existed on some campuses with high levels of prevention education but few avenues to restrict access and availability of alcohol. Some of the tier three strategies that show promise yet require more comprehensive evaluation and may be effective among the Millennial college student population include eliminating keg parties on campus; establishing alcohol-free dormitories; employing older, salaried resident assistants or hiring adults to fulfill that role;

further controlling or eliminating alcohol at sports events and prohibiting tailgating parties that model heavy alcohol use; refusing sponsorship gifts from the alcohol industry to avoid any perception that underage drinking is acceptable; and banning alcohol on campus, including at faculty and alumni events. Other tier three strategies include reducing mixed messages about alcohol use on campus, consistently enforcing policies and disciplinary actions, using social marketing to change student perceptions of alcohol use on campus, creating safe ride programs, regulating alcohol specials, and educating students and parents about alcohol policies prior to matriculation.

While these strategies have been identified by the NIAAA as methods to curb high-risk alcohol use, it is equally important—and with the Millennial generation entering college, becoming increasingly important—to create an environment that supports students who consistently make low-risk choices. To fulfill this effort, it is essential to have strong community partnerships that foster consistent messaging on campus and in the community. This combines policies to promote low-risk behavior, such as parental notification, "solid" discipline policies, ID laws, and consistent enforcement as well as education about all of these issues.

> "Many Yale students liberally engage in behaviors such as making out, giving or receiving oral sex, and having intercourse."

The College "Hookup" Culture Is Widespread

Emily Foxhall

Emily Foxhall is a contributing reporter to the Yale Daily News, *a daily college newspaper that has been in circulation since 1878. The following viewpoint appeared as one of a series of articles published during "Sex Week at Yale," an interdisciplinary campus program designed to spark interest and open dialogue about sexual health topics. Foxhall discusses the results of a survey conducted at Yale by the newspaper regarding students' sexual activity and romantic expectations. The results reveal a "hookup" culture, involving frequent physical relationships that generally lack the emotional investment between partners that typifies traditional romantic pairings.*

As you read, consider the following questions:

1. According to Foxhall, how do the Yale survey results compare to a similar poll conducted at Harvard?

2. What survey results does Foxhall mention that suggest that Yale men set the tone for sexual relationships?

3. In the author's view, why are many Yale students content with non-emotional sexual relationships?

It's Monday morning. You are in a seminar with 20 class-mates, half men, half women. In the past week, about six of them have had sexual intercourse. The same goes for oral sex. Half of them have made out with someone. All but one or two of the men have masturbated. By comparison, only about four of the women masturbated in the past week. Roughly eight people in the class used their hands to sexually stimulate someone else. How students found time to do the reading for class is anyone's guess.

This scenario was an estimate of Yale's sexscape based on the results of a *Yale Daily News* poll, sent last week [early February 2010] to 5,186 undergraduates, of which 1,770 students responded. The poll reveals a tendency toward regular sexual activity, part of a hookup culture that many students interviewed said defines Yale's sex scene.

Hookup Culture

Yalies don't like to fail, and that goes for their sex lives, too. The quest for sexual gratification leads many—but not all—students to seek casual hookups, in an environment that most Elis [Yale students] interviewed said promotes carnal interaction over cultivated relationships. According to the *News*'s poll, the median Yale senior has had sexual intercourse with two people but only one relationship since the beginning of his or her freshman year. The poll and separate interviews with students showed that many Yale students liberally engage in behaviors such as making out, giving or receiving oral sex, and having intercourse. "The interactions between guys and girls [at Yale] are now more often hookups than dates," Robby Wyper [class of] '13 said. "I don't really know anything different."

Over the course of [his or her] Yale career, the median Yale senior has made out with eight different people. Ninety percent of all Yale students have made out with someone at some point, while 75.3 percent have engaged in oral sex with someone, and 64.3 percent have had sexual intercourse.

A poll by the *Harvard Crimson* in May 2009 showed that the median Harvard senior has had one sexual partner by the end of his or her senior year. By comparison, the median Yale student has had sexual intercourse with two partners, and oral sex with three partners, the *News*'s poll results showed.

Lori Santos, a psychology professor who studies evolutionary biology by comparing the cognitive abilities of human and non-human primates and teaches the popular "Psychology of Sex" course, said random hookups are an unnatural phenomenon, given that humans naturally tend toward forming relationship pairs. Humans are genetically wired to crave sex so as to pass on their genes, she said, which explains their ability to derive physical pleasure from sex. But with the rise of contraceptives, she said, this evolutionary explanation gets complicated because sex no longer always leads to procreation, allowing females to be less choosy when finding sexual partners. "Historically, there was always a link between having sex and bearing children," she said, but now things have changed. "You can engage in these behaviors without having the consequence of having a baby."

Work Hard, Play Hard

The pervasive hookup culture at Yale is promoted by the ease with which casual encounters fit into the academic rigor of Yale, students said. "Hookups, by virtue of the academic environment that we are in, are much easier and much more sustainable," Michael Jones '12 said. "I guess by extension of the environments we are in, when you're interacting at a party, it's very difficult to develop a meaningful, emotional relationship with someone immediately."

As explained by Sarah Matthes '13, a large portion of this pattern can potentially be attributed to what is commonly referred to as "DFMO," short for dance-floor makeout. Citing Safety Dance, fraternity parties and Modern Love [campus events] as common hookup venues, she described kissing as "trivial" in the light of questions pertaining to intercourse and oral sex. Even at Toad's Place [nightclub] or a campus party, kissing someone is considered a dance move.

"Here I think making out is something that can happen and people can wake up the next morning and laugh about it and go about their day," she said, while admitting that there is a separate contingency of Yale students who did not participate in frivolous makeout sessions at all. About nine percent of students polled reported to have never made out with anyone.

"From a single guy's point of view, I find few things more fun than going out at night and seeing what I can come home with," Wyper said. "It's fun. It's exciting. I'm not looking to fill my empty heart. Wednesday through Saturday you have a pretty decent shot at hooking up with somebody." He added that many men hope a hookup will lead to intercourse, but many women may feel differently.

According to the poll, 19.5 percent of Yale men have never engaged in oral sex, compared to 29.1 percent of women. Similarly, the poll showed that 30.5 percent of Yale men have never had intercourse, compared to 40.2 percent of women. Jaqueline Erickson '10 said Yale's hookup culture frequently allows men to set the tone for sexual relationships, and in turn, women often sacrifice their desire for an emotional attachment. "As much as I feel like the sexual culture at Yale is disrespectful to women, I feel like females don't live by higher expectations," she said. "They're going back to guys who treat them awful."

Josh Ruck '13 said a hookup crescendos when a random makeout leads to casual sex. The signal for this transition is often the girl inviting the guy back to her room, or vice versa, he said. "Most of the girls know why they're taking a boy back," Ruck said.

According to the poll, 31.2 percent of students have performed or received oral sex within the last week, and 28.5 percent of students have had intercourse within the last week. This surprised Matthes and several other students interviewed; Matthes said she believed many girls often refused to participate in oral sex but would consent to intercourse. "I think that's also a tricky situation because oral sex can be seen as degrading," Matthes said. "I think that makes people a little less inclined to engage in it. It's also just difficult for people. It's not something that comes naturally or easily. It's intimidating."

Sexually Frustrated

Though many students participate in Yale's pervasive hookup culture, many Yalies are frustrated by it, students interviewed said, adding that they only settle for it begrudgingly. "I think that very few people are actually legitimately happy with the way things are. I sincerely think that," Ann Chou '10 said. "I don't think very many people are satisfied." She said much of this dissatisfaction stems from the fact that many Yalies have not thought through what they want to gain from their Yale weekends. Jones said it is ironic that Yale students presumably have impressive academic intelligence, yet fail to analyze their own feelings when it comes to relationships.

While some sexual activity at Yale is purely carnal, some occurs with the underlying hope held by one or both partners that it will eventually evolve into a relationship in the more traditional sense of the term, Jones said. "There are a lot of people who are together in that they hook up all the time," Jones said. "But there's very little emotional investment. It's a wonder that we've passed that off as a relationship, but that is as close as most of us get." While Ruck said both parties often

Familiarity Between the Sexes Kills Romance and Marriage

In the new culture that our colleges incubate and maintain, everyone is a "guy." Everyone is "familiar." Young men and women who have never seen anyone of the opposite sex naked or in underwear, other than family members, now must get used to being seen by and seeing others—perfect strangers—in just such a state. Everyone is available to everyone else. It would be antisocial not to be.

Under such conditions, how could dating and courtship possibly survive? How could traditional marriage survive, in the long term? Courtship and dating require an inviolable private space from which each sex can leave at appointed times to meet in public and enjoy the other. In other words, in a courtship culture it ought to be that two people who are "serious" actually do "go out" together and do not merely cohabit in a closeted dormitory or apartment. Yet over the past 40 years, American colleges have created a brave new unisex world in which distinctions between public and private, formal and familiar, have collapsed. The differences between the sexes are now dangerously minimized or else just plain ignored because to recognize them is not progressive or politically correct. This is manifestly the case with coed dorm floors and shared bathrooms and showers. These give the lie to official college rules against cohabitation. They are the wink and nod our colleges give to fornication and dissipation. Even in 1957, when he was chancellor of the University of California at Berkeley, Clark Kerr was almost prophetic when he stated humorously that his job responsibilities were "providing parking for faculty, sex for students, and athletics for the alumni."

Vigen Guroian, "Dorm Brothel,"
Christianity Today, *February 2005.*

entertain the possibility of a relationship, he also said he knows of several guys who had led girls to believe they were more interested in a real relationship than they actually were in order to prolong the hookup. On the flip side, he said girls have also been known to have sex with guys with the sole hope that it will help keep them around. But he said many hookups end the moment the girl says, "I want to be exclusive."

Chou also addressed how many Yale students begin to value themselves based on their grades or their number of leadership positions, and they have a hard time entering into relationships because the time they require, especially in college, takes away from these other activities. Because Yalies are often strapped for time, Chou said, they fear the potential burden of a relationship, as well as the repercussions of a breakup.

Still, for those students unconcerned with relationships, Yale's hookup culture can offer the physical satisfaction students seek—both consciously and subconsciously.

Ruck maintained that, when it comes to sex at Yale, "If you want it, it's there. At the end of the day, you can get laid. . . . You're not forced to see them on a daily basis so you can get away with it. People don't care about the consequences and don't think about it."

> *"When it comes to actual sexual activity, statistics show that coeds are more likely to be virgins when they enter college, and may be having slightly less sex than in previous years."*

The College "Hookup" Culture Is Exaggerated by the Media

Jennie Yabroff

Jennie Yabroff is a writer for Newsweek *magazine. In the following viewpoint, Yabroff discusses the impression that colleges give—that campuses are running rampant with random hookups and casual sex. When it comes down to actual sexual activity, however, the statistics point the opposite way. The decline in sexual activity among college coeds can be attributed to increased awareness of sexually transmitted diseases, according to the article.*

As you read, consider the following questions:

1. The author claims that sex magazines and journals are gaining popularity even though no increase in sexual activity among college students has occurred. What is one reason given as to why this is the case?

Jennie Yabroff, "Campus Sexperts: Erotic Magazines Run by Students at Elite Colleges Have Prospered. So Why Are They Having Less Sex?" *Newsweek*, February 16, 2008. Reproduced by permission.

2. According to a 2001 study cited in the article, what percentage of female college freshmen were virgins?

3. What is one of the reasons Yabroff gives for the decline in sexual activity on college campuses?

As the writer of a blog called Sex and the Ivy, Harvard student Lena Chen promotes herself as something of an authority on sex. The 20-year-old sociology major is a minor celebrity around campus for her musings on hookups, booty calls and friends with benefits. So Chen, as self-appointed poster girl for what could be called a group of brainy girls gone wild, was an obvious choice to document a week's worth of conquests for a national magazine's online sex diary. Except for the tallies at the end of the week: Total acts of intercourse? Zero.

The Paradox of Modern College Life

Chen says she's since broken her dry spell, but the episode illustrates a paradox of modern college life: Students are publicly documenting their sex lives more than ever, making it easy to get the impression that elite campuses are an equivalent of the sex club in *Eyes Wide Shut*, with a perfect SAT score as the password. But when it comes to actual sexual activity, statistics show that coeds are more likely to be virgins when they enter college, and may be having slightly less sex than in previous years. Despite this, blogs such as Chen's, student-paper sex columns, student-run sex magazines like Harvard's *H Bomb*, Yale's *SWAY* (an acronym for Sex Week at Yale) and Boston University's *Boink* have proliferated. As Dr. Jeanne Brooks-Gunn, codirector of the National Center for Children and Families, says, "What's interesting is, why are these journals gaining such popularity even though you're not seeing a big increase in sexual activity among college students?" One answer is that in an era of online exposure, where changing definitions of privacy have shifted sexual mores for the young, enterprising students no longer see a distinction between their bedroom behavior and their publishing activities. Rather than something to destroy upon graduation, they may even consider their magazines, blogs and columns résumé builders.

Apparently, when it comes to sex, write what you know doesn't always apply. "Everyone assumes because of the magazine that I'm sleeping with everything that walks," says Alecia Oleyourryk, editor of Boston University's *Boink*, who posed nude for the first issue. The magazine claims 40,000 subscribers, and has spawned the new book *Boink: College Sex by the People Having It*. "It's not the case. Respective to my girlfriends, I'm the most prudish." Oleyourryk's comments reflect the findings of a new survey by the American College Health Association [ACHA]. When asked to estimate how many sexual partners their peers had had during the past school year, college students guessed three times the number of partners they'd had. "Even people involved in extreme behavior think their friends are more extreme," says Kathleen Bogle, author of *Hooking Up: Sex, Dating, and Relationships on Campus*. The study also found that for male students, the number of sexual partners in the previous year has dropped, from 2.1 in 2000 to 1.6 in 2006. According to a Centers for Disease Control survey, the number of ninth- to 12th-grade students who have had sex dropped almost 10 percent, to fewer than half of respondents, between 1991 and 2005. And a 2001 study found that 39 percent of freshman college women were virgins, and 31 percent of those women still hadn't had sex by senior year. In 2006, nearly half of Harvard undergrads who responded to a survey reported they had never had intercourse.

Reasons for Decline in Hookups

The slight decline may be explained by increased awareness of the potential downsides of sex, such as STDs [sexually transmitted diseases] or on-campus abstinence movements such as Harvard's True Love Revolution student group, says [E.] Victor Leino, research director for the ACHA. Still, students involved in sex publications say there's a need for more conversation about the intricacies and emotions regarding sex, regardless of how much of it they're actually having. Jenna Bromberg, a Cornell senior who writes a sex column for the school paper, says she wants to spur discussion of the pluses and minuses of hooking up. "A lot of the time I put gross stories in there to get people talking," she says. While Martabel Wasserman, the editor of *H Bomb*, takes a less confessional approach, she agrees that "there is a hole in our dialogue about sexuality. The idea is that it's a very free time, but it's also a very scary time." After a three-year hiatus due to administrative troubles, *H Bomb* will resume publishing next month.

These publications are not purely academic exercises: their creators hope they lead to professional opportunities after graduation. "People think it's a stigma, but I think we're in changing times, and it can open doors for me," says Oleyourryk, who recently moved to New York and is looking for work as a waitress while she continues publishing *Boink*. "I continually tell my mom this is a great résumé builder," she says, though she's vague about what she'll use her résumé for. Though the young sexpert's optimism may seem naïve, it's not necessarily misguided, says Pepper Schwartz, a sociologist at the University of Washington. "Maybe their generation will take this a lot less seriously than we do," she says. In the age of MySpace and Facebook, sex may be just one more way to network. "To me, talking about sex and one-night stands is superficial. What I keep out of the column is the intimate stuff," says Bromberg, adding that she wouldn't write about a serious relationship.

The students' cavalier attitudes may stem from confidence about their futures fostered by the elite institutions they use as publishing platforms. "A lot of these Ivy League students are bright, self-confident, and they have some extra money to get these things started," says Schwartz. "Whether their class origins are protecting them, or giving them more license, I don't know, but class always has an impact." Certainly, the students behind the publications are earnest and articulate, and may be able to land the jobs of their dreams. If they do experience misgivings about their activities, it may be for personal reasons. "The only times I regret writing the column," says Bromberg, "is when I have to look my dad in the eye."

> *"Three hours after taking it, I started shaking. I felt like my heart was bouncing out of my body. I lost my appetite. I couldn't sleep for a full two days. It was a nightmare."*

Adderall Is a Dangerous, Addictive Drug

Megan Twohey

Megan Twohey is a metro reporter at the Chicago Tribune *newspaper; she previously wrote for the* Milwaukee Journal Sentinel. *The following viewpoint discusses how college students use the drug Adderall, a prescription drug for attention deficit hyperactivity disorder (ADHD), which can improve concentration and focus even for people not affected by the symptoms of ADHD. Many students acquire pills illegally and take advantage of the mental effects as a study aid, Twohey points out. Adderall is an amphetamine, and she asserts that users are at risk for becoming dependent on it. Without the supervision of a doctor, students who take the drugs put themselves in real physical danger.*

As you read, consider the following questions:

1. What are some side effects of Adderall use, as described by Twohey?
2. Why, according to Davis Smith, is so much Adderall available on college campuses?
3. According to Eric Heiligenstein, what are some psychological contributions to Adderall dependence?

A tough math class prompted Rich to take the drug. The effect: "I could study for, like, eight hours straight," said the University of Wisconsin [UW]-Madison junior. Samantha, a Marquette University sophomore, popped it on the eve of a big history test. "I stayed up all night," she said, "and totally zoned in."

For years, students have used coffee, NoDoz caffeine pills and other stimulants to help them through exams, papers and other demands of college.

Today, some students are taking a study aid that can be deadly.

Adderall, a medication for attention deficit hyperactivity disorder, or ADHD, has become popular among college students who don't have the disorder, according to students, college health officials and an emerging body of research. Adderall is an amphetamine and works like cocaine. Those who use it can stay focused and awake for hours on end. Students with prescriptions sell it or give it away.

"If you can take a drug that allows you to stay awake through finals week and concentrate on relatively boring topics, you can see how the word would spread," said William Frankenberger, a psychology professor at UW-Eau Claire. He led a 2004 survey of students on a UW campus that found 14% had abused Adderall or another ADHD medication.

But using the drug without a prescription is dangerous. The federal government has classified Adderall under the same category as cocaine, opium and morphine, drugs with a high potential for abuse. It is illegal to sell it or use it without a prescription.

Side effects include insomnia, irritability and loss of appetite. In extreme cases, the drug can cause paranoia, hallucinations and heart attacks. Adderall and other ADHD medications have been reportedly linked to the deaths of 25 people in recent years. U.S. Food and Drug Administration advisers are recommending warnings on the drugs' labels.

The Prevalence of Adderall

Between the 1940s and 1970s, before their addictive properties were known, amphetamines were used to treat obesity, fatigue and depression, according to a 2005 report from the National Center on Addiction and Substance Abuse. Pilots used the stimulant during World War II to stay awake. Dieters used it to lose weight rapidly.

In the 1990s, amphetamines re-emerged. A growing number of children were being diagnosed with ADHD, a neurobehavioral disorder that makes people hyperactive and incapable of concentrating. Adderall and Ritalin, an amphetamine-like drug, were among the medications that were approved as effective treatments.

Between 1992 and 2002, the number of prescriptions for ADHD medications in the U.S. increased 369% to 23.4 million a year, according to the National Center on Addiction and Substance Abuse report.

In 2005, there were 31.8 million prescriptions for such medications, according to IMS Health, a pharmaceutical information and consulting company. The most popular was Adderall.

Colleges are now seeing waves of students who grew up on ADHD medication.

Some of the students don't need it, said Davis Smith, director of student health at Wesleyan University in Connecticut, who has been gathering information about the use of ADHD medication for the American College Health Association.

Smith said aggressive pharmaceutical marketing campaigns and pressure from pushy parents have caused doctors to over-prescribe the drugs.

Eric Heiligenstein, clinical director of psychiatry at UW-Madison's health services, agreed.

"We have students who come in and say they got it just asking for it at other clinics," he said.

When they don't need it, some students misuse their medication. So do students who are wary of becoming dependent. Instead of taking it twice a day, as often prescribed, these students only take it around exam time or in other high-pressure situations.

In 2000, UW-Madison surveyed 100 students with prescriptions for ADHD medication. It found that one in five misused the prescription regularly.

That has created opportunities for other students to get the medication, Heiligenstein said. Students with excess pills are often willing to sell them or give them away.

Abuse at Competitive Schools

A survey of students at 119 colleges nationwide found that, on certain campuses, up to 25% of respondents had misused ADHD medication in the past year. The survey, published last year [2005] in the journal *Addiction*, found that rates were highest at colleges that were competitive, those in the Northeast and those with high rates of binge drinking. Students with grade point averages [GPAs] of B or lower were two times more likely to use the drugs than students earning a B+ or higher.

Angie, a UW-Madison junior, said it's common for students to get Adderall from friends. She has paid $5 for a couple of pills. At other times, friends have given her the drug for free. "Doctors are just handing it out," said Adam, a freshman at Marquette. "Friends are willing to give it away."

Doctors are supposed to review a student's medical history before prescribing ADHD medication. That's to make sure that they won't have a heart attack or another extreme reaction. Students who get Adderall from friends have no idea how their bodies will react. Those interviewed for this story have had varied reactions.

Adam, the Marquette freshman, said Adderall gave him the energy to stay up all night. It also changed his attitude. "It's almost like you enjoy the work," he said. But the next day, he felt like he had an extreme hangover.

The effect on Rachel, a senior at UW-Madison, was much worse. "Three hours after taking it, I started shaking," she said. "I felt like my heart was bouncing out of my body. I lost my appetite. I couldn't sleep for a full two days. It was a nightmare."

Rich, the UW-Madison junior, has taken Adderall for two years to study for tests. During that time, his grades have improved. Today, he feels dependent.

UW-Madison's health center is seeing a growing number of cases like his. "We see a blend of psychological and physical dependence," Heiligenstein said. "Students take it, get better results and feel like they can't go off. They say—I feel like I've built my whole GPA on this. How can I stop?"

Critics worry the drug is now being used like an academic steroid, creating an unfair playing field on college campuses. But not everyone is popping it.

"I'll stick with caffeine," said Amanda Rosen, a freshman at UW-Madison, as she walked into the campus library, a chai tea in hand. "That way I'll know that I'm getting the grade."

| "Taking Ritalin before an exam is no different from eating well or getting enough sleep."

Cognitive-Enhancing Drugs Are Useful Study Aids

Anne McIlroy

Anne McIlroy is the science reporter for the Globe and Mail; *she has also reported on political topics. The following viewpoint addresses the controversial subject of cognitive-enhancing drugs, such as Ritalin and Adderall, which were designed to help people with attention deficit hyperactivity disorder (ADHD) concentrate but end up being used by students who want a boost while studying or before taking a test. McIlroy reports on a study published in the journal* Nature *in which the authors discuss cognitive-enhancing drugs as a tool no less legitimate than getting a good night's sleep to rest the brain or taking caffeine to help it focus.*

As you read, consider the following questions:

1. With what generally accepted hobbies and personal enrichment activities does Tim Caulfield group the use of cognitive-enhancing drugs?

2. According to the article in *Nature* cited by McIlroy, why is the use of cognitive-enhancing drugs by scholars and students potentially more beneficial than the use of performance-enhancing drugs by athletes?

3. What level of intelligence does Michael Minzenberg say is best served by taking cognitive-enhancing drugs?

Your son is in his final year of high school and says some of the other students are taking Ritalin to help them concentrate while they study and write exams.

The drug may help him get into the university of his choice or win a scholarship. He wants to try it. What do you say?

Surveys suggest that in the United States, an increasing number of healthy university students are using so-called cognitive-enhancing drugs such as Ritalin and modafinil to improve their academic performance. One found that on some campuses, as many as one in four students used these kinds of drugs to get better marks, and that overall 7 per cent had done so.

The trend is likely to spread, experts say. In this week's [December 12, 2008] edition of the journal *Nature*, a group of scientists and ethicists say it's time we all started thinking about the benefits of healthy individuals taking drugs to boost their brain power.

Cognitive-Enhancing Drug Use Isn't "Cheating"

Many people consider the non-medical use of these kinds of drugs to be cheating, in the same way that athletes who take performance-enhancing drugs are breaking the rules.

But in their commentary in *Nature*, Stanford University's Henry Greely and his colleagues argue that taking Ritalin before an exam is no different from eating well or getting enough sleep.

Illicit Use of Prescription ADHD Medications among College Students

Demographic	Using		Not using	
	n	%	n	%
Overall	585	34	1,148	66
Sex				
Male	278	39	430	61
Female	266	30	629	70
Race				
White/Caucasian	547	35	1,032	65
Other Race/Ethnicity	34	25	101	75
Year in School				
Freshman	101	18	473	82
Sophomore	127	31	288	69
Junior	144	49	150	51
Senior	137	55	112	45
Greek Status				
No	228	23	747	77
Yes	357	48	389	52

Note: ADHD = Attention deficit hyperactivity disorder.

TAKEN FROM: Alan DeSantis et al., "Illicit Use of Prescription ADHD Medications on a College Campus," *Journal of American College Health*, 2008.

The seven authors, from the United States and Britain, include ethics experts and the editor in chief of *Nature* as well as scientists. They developed their case at a seminar funded by *Nature* and the Rockefeller University in New York. Two authors said they consult for pharmaceutical companies. The others reported no such financial ties.

"Recent research has identified beneficial neural changes engendered by exercise, nutrition and sleep. In short, cognitive-enhancing drugs seem morally equivalent to other, more familiar enhancements," they argue in the commentary.

It is not an uncommon view among experts who have considered the ethical issues surrounding these drugs.

"Normally, our society reveres self-improvement," says Tim Caulfield, Canada Research Chair in Health Law and Policy at the University of Alberta.

"Doing yoga? Good for you. Taking guitar lessons? Impressive. Learning a new language? How mind-expanding. Speed reading lessons? Nice. Cognitive enhancers? You unworthy cheaters," Dr. Caulfield says.

Putting aside the issue of whether these drugs are safe when used in this manner, he says, it is tough to come up with reasons why taking them should be banned. "Even though they seem like 'cheating,' in what qualitative way are they different from other forms of enhancement? Coffee is an enhancer. Should students be banned from using it before an exam?" All education is pharmacological, Dr. Caulfield says. "Learning changes brain chemistry."

But isn't allowing some students to use the drugs while others don't similar to giving only half the people in a class calculators for a math exam? Dr. Greely and his colleagues argue that this kind of unfairness already exists.

"Differences in education, including private tutoring, preparatory courses and other enriching experiences give some students an advantage over others," they write.

Scientists Report Using Cognitive-Enhancing Drugs

The question of whether these drugs work remains unanswered, but there is evidence that many scientists and academics think they do.

Earlier this year [2008], the journal *Nature* published the results of an online poll that asked readers if they were using drugs such as Ritalin to improve their performance. About 20 per cent of the 1,400 respondents said they had tried to improve their memory, concentration and focus by taking drugs for non-medical reasons.

They were asked about the following: Ritalin (also known as methylphenidate), a stimulant used to treat attention deficit hyperactivity disorder; modafinil (sold under the brand name Provigil), offered by doctors as a treatment for sleep disorders but also used "off-label" to fight fatigue and jet lag; and beta blockers, which are usually prescribed to treat irregular heartbeats but can reduce anxiety. Ritalin was the most popular.

The people who read *Nature* are mainly academics and scientists, and 5.5 per cent who participated in the survey were from Canada.

Half of those who took the drugs said they obtained them through prescriptions, while a third said they ordered them over the Internet and 14 per cent said they bought them at a drugstore.

Learning more about how the drugs work might lead to greater acceptance of people taking them for non-medical reasons, Dr. Greely and his colleagues say.

If these medications improve long-term learning, they offer the potential of new discoveries and innovations, they write in *Nature*. You can't say that about an athlete taking steroids to win Olympic gold.

While scientists understand how steroids help build muscles, they don't know why these drugs may hone mental prowess in healthy individuals.

In this week's edition of the journal *Science*, Michael Minzenberg, with the department of psychiatry at the University of California, Davis, and his colleagues offer the first glimpse of what modafinil does in the human brain.

Brain scans of people who had taken the drug showed a decided shift in their mental state; they went from being easily distracted to being in "the zone," and more focused on a task,

Dr. Minzenberg says. But he says he doesn't take it himself or prescribe it to healthy individuals.

"I don't do that under any circumstances."

The Benefits Are Limited

Evidence suggests drugs such as this one would do more to help people of low to normal intelligence than individuals with high IQs, he says.

As for long-term effects, he notes, a four-year study that followed patients taking modafinil for narcolepsy showed no significant problems or signs that it was addictive.

Still, safety remains a big issue, and the academics who wrote the commentary piece in *Nature* call for more research into how the drugs affect healthy individuals.

Using any drug carries a risk. The online survey conducted by *Nature* found that half of those who had used cognitive-enhancing drugs reported unpleasant side effects, including headaches, trouble sleeping, or feeling jittery or anxious. Other side effects of Ritalin include dizziness, nausea, vomiting, diarrhea, chest pain and shortness of breath. Modafinil can cause constipation, sweating, itchiness, mouth sores and hives.

So what do you tell a son or daughter who wants to take drugs to get better marks?

"This is a tough one," Dr. Caulfield says. "As a parent of four kids, this is my biggest concern—especially if they don't have the safety issues nailed down.

"But I tell my kids to get a good sleep before a big test. I tell them to have a good breakfast. I tell them to study. All of these are enhancement activities."

Periodical Bibliography

The following articles have been selected to supplement the diverse views presented in this chapter.

Robin Acton · "Many Say Little Has Changed at Penn State Since Alcohol-Related Death," *Tribune-Review* (Pittsburgh, PA), October 25, 2009.

Jennifer Epstein · "Campus Drinking: Colleges' Problem, or Society's?" *USA Today*, June 4, 2010.

Cody Howard · "Professor Sheds Light on Prevalence of Texting and Driving," University of Kansas, April 28, 2010. www.news.ku.edu.

Barbara Alvarez Martin et al. · "The Role of Monthly Spending Money in College Student Drinking Behaviors and Their Consequences," *Journal of American College Health*, 2009.

Alan Mozes · "1 in 5 College Students Admitted to Drunk Driving, Study Found," HealthDay, June 2, 2010. http://consumer.healthday.com.

Rachael Rettner · "Going Tanning as Addictive as Drinking: 1 in 3 College Students Who Tan Could Be Hooked, Study Says," MSNBC, April 19, 2010. www.msnbc.msn.com.

Larry Truong · "UF Students Taking Fitness Supplements to Get in Shape Faster," *Gainesville Sun* (Florida), February 9, 2010.

Brian J. Willoughby and Jason S. Carroll · "The Impact of Living in Co-Ed Resident Halls on Risk-Taking Among College Students," *Journal of American College Health*, November–December 2009.

Alan Scher Zagier · "'Shot Books' Record 21st Birthday Binges," *Virginian-Pilot* (Norfolk, VA), February 28, 2010.

OPPOSING
VIEWPOINTS®
SERIES

CHAPTER 2

Do Students Receive Adequate Health Care on Campus?

Chapter Preface

In 2009, Clemson University junior Danielle Fleming died very suddenly from bacterial meningitis. Bacterial meningitis is rare, but it kills 15 percent of its victims; and college students, particularly freshmen living in dormitories on campus, are more likely to contract it than people in other age groups. The United States Advisory Committee on Immunization Practices recommended in 2007 the routine vaccination of teenagers and young adults against the disease, but only a handful of states have enacted laws requiring college students to be immunized; and many states do not even require schools to educate students about the transmission and symptoms of the disease. After Fleming's death, Clemson made vaccination against meningitis a requirement for enrollment, a policy that many other colleges have also put into place.

Universal vaccination programs are quite prevalent among younger students, but immunization rates fall off in the late teens and throughout adulthood. Even when states like New York pass laws requiring college students to be vaccinated against mumps before enrolling, outbreaks still occur. The on-campus residential environment of shared bedrooms, bathrooms, and dining halls encourages the spread of germs, and college students who work and study hard are not as able to fight off infections as people who are less stressed and tired. In addition, college health centers are not equipped to handle many cases of illness at once.

As a result, colleges often take extreme measures to stop the spread of infectious disease through the student body. During the H1N1 outbreaks in 2009, swine flu cases were seen among university students right at the beginning of the school year, well before vaccines were widely available. Anxious to prevent widespread contamination, schools resorted to unusual restrictions on students' freedoms. Rensselaer Polytechnic Institute in New York banned drinking games (generally played with communal cups); Mount Holyoke College in Massachusetts drove sick students home by car; Pennsylvania State University kept ailing students out of cafeterias and delivered boxed meals to their rooms. Emory University in Georgia went even further: It designated an entire dormitory as a sickroom and quarantined up to one hundred students inside until they recovered. Students were locked in isolation from the rest of campus, visited by only a few staff members to bring groceries or clean bedding and driven to their doctor appointments in a special van. Enforced involuntary quarantine is very rare in the United States and legally tricky, but Emory (and other schools employing quarantine and isolation tactics) implemented quarantine without any political ramifications.

Vaccination requirements and quarantine plans are community health measures that value group welfare above personal freedom. Colleges and universities ask students to sacrifice personal freedom for the benefit of the health of the student body far more often than is asked of adults outside the school setting. On the one hand, a college is an organization that has the right to determine the conditions under which students will be allowed to enroll; on the other hand, most schools accept government funding and must comply with national rules about rights and privileges guaranteed to persons by law. Schools are not allowed to discriminate against students according to race, sex, age, or sexual orientation, but they have the power to dictate what medical treatments students must accept before participating in their programs. Clemson can insist that an eighteen-year-old who wants to live on campus must accept the meningitis vaccine and its risks; the manager of an apartment building in the same city evaluating an eighteen-year-old prospective tenant cannot.

While there are certain risks and costs associated with mandatory vaccination policies, many universities assert that such policies are worth the financial and administrative costs,

As you read, consider the following questions:

1. What university received the only perfect score according to the Trojan Sexual Health Report Card?

2. According to the article, what percentage of schools has a sex advice column in a school paper or online?

3. What school in the top ten was the only university to receive a grade of B?

Many college students may be left ill-informed about safer sex and more at risk for sexually transmitted infections (STIs) and unintended pregnancies because of a lack of access to information about sexual health and availability of condoms at some schools, according to the Trojan Sexual Health Report Card—released today from the makers of Trojan brand condoms and Sperling's Best Places—which is the first survey that grades the sexual health of colleges and universities across the country and ranks them. Despite this, many schools were found to do a good job of providing essential information about sexual health to students, which put them at the top of the list.

Yale University, for example, received the only perfect score and was found to have excellent resources for students. Yale also holds the annual Sex Week at Yale (SWAY), which promotes open on-campus discussion of sex and relationships, and makes information about sexual health easily accessible online and through the student health center.

Other schools in the top 10 that were also shown to provide easily accessible sexual health resources to students were the University of Iowa (#2), University of Michigan—Ann Arbor (#3), Stanford University (#4), Oregon State University (#5), Princeton University (#6), University of New Hampshire (#7), Duke University (#8), Ohio State University (#9) and University of Illinois (#10).

Schools at the bottom of the list were the University of Nevada (#91), followed by University of Wyoming (#92),

Reported Cases of Sexually Transmitted Diseases Rates among College-Age Adolescents and Young Adults

Age Group	Chlamydia	Gonorrhea	Syphilis	Year
15–19	323,246	87,454	339	2004
20–24	344,159	103,187	1,029	
15–19	336,036	90,840	443	2005
20–24	360,574	106,280	1,181	
15–19	352,212	96,524	565	2006
20–24	377,798	110,969	1,382	
15–19	379,416	98,579	664	2007
20–24	402,597	111,788	1,818	
15–19	420,101	97,293	903	2008
20–24	438,311	109,005	2,398	

TAKEN FROM: *Sexually Transmitted Disease Surveillance 2008*, Centers for Disease Control and Prevention, November 2009.

University of Louisville (#93), Texas Tech University (#94), Clemson University (#95), University of Memphis (#96), Oklahoma State University (#97), University of Utah (#98), University of Notre Dame (#99), and Brigham Young University (#100).

The Need for Sexual Health Information

The Trojan Sexual Health Report Card looked at 100 public and private schools, at least one from every state. Sperling examined various criteria, including resources about sexual health, the depth of information available on the school's Web site and the availability of condoms on campus, to determine a school's score, which was calculated in the same manner as a student's grade point average.

"We live in a country with the highest rates of new STIs and unintended pregnancies of any Western nation, and we applaud those schools that provide fact-based, accurate and comprehensive information about sexual health to all students," said Jim Daniels, Vice President [of] Marketing for Trojan condoms. "While we understand there are a variety of reasons some schools do not provide these resources to students, we feel that comprehensive education and access to information is the best way to ensure people make smart decisions about protection should they choose to be sexually active."

Bert Sperling looked at resources available to students in order to determine the rankings. "In our research, we put ourselves in the place of a student seeking information about sexual health, and we found it difficult to find this type of information at a range of colleges throughout the country," said Bert Sperling of Sperling's Best Places. "There is an immense divide between those schools that offer comprehensive, fact-based sexual health resources to students and provide a forum for discussion of related topics, and those where, for a variety of reasons, information is difficult to come by."

Key findings included:

- 93 percent of schools surveyed offer some type of STI testing to students—with 24 percent offering free testing on campus.

- Only 32 percent of schools have a sex advice column online or in the school paper.

- With the exception of Oregon State University, which received a grade of B, all schools in the top 10 received an A in the Web site category which measures ease of access to information about sexual health on the school's Web site.

- 76 percent of schools surveyed do not provide free condoms to students.

- The average score for schools in the top 10 was 3.49, compared with an average of .43 for schools in the bottom 10.

While the top and bottom 10 schools in the survey are regionally diverse, the Northeast does show a slight edge over other regions:

- 20 percent of schools in the Northeast received a 3.0 score or better.

- 10.5 percent of schools in the Midwest received a 3.0 score or better.

- 10.3 percent of schools in the West received a 3.0 score or better.

- 7.4 percent of schools in the South received a 3.0 or better.

- Regional breakdown of schools: 29 schools from the West, 27 schools from the South, 25 schools from the Northeast and 19 schools from the Midwest.

"We know that 18- to 24-year-olds use condoms only for one in four sex acts, and we believe that it is important for those who choose to be sexually active and are at risk for STIs to understand the risks, and use a condom for every sex act," said Daniels. "With this survey, we hope to shine a light on the need for greater discussion about these issues, which can help lead to lower rates of infection and unintended pregnancies."

This year in the United States, it is estimated that almost 19 million people will be diagnosed with an STI, and there will be more than 3 million unintended pregnancies. Currently, there are 65 million Americans living with an incurable STI.

About Trojan

Trojan brand condoms are America's #1 condom and have been trusted for nearly 90 years. Trojan brand latex condoms are made from premium quality latex to help reduce the risk of unwanted pregnancy and sexually transmitted diseases. Each condom is electronically tested to help ensure reliability. There are over 29 varieties of Trojan brand condoms. More Americans trust the Trojan brand than any other condom.

About Sperling's Best Places

For over 16 years, Bert Sperling has been analyzing data about people and places and rating them for major publications. Sperling's concepts and methodology have been the basis of numerous studies since 1985, when he developed a software program named "Places, U.S.A." that allowed people to enter their personal preferences to find their own best place. Today, his company, Fast Forward, Inc. (the producer of BestPlaces.net) is responsible for more "Best Places" studies and projects than any other organization. His Web site, Best Places.net, provides accurate and up-to-date information about demographics, preferences, and the selection of "Best Places" to live, work, or retire, in a useful and entertaining format.

About the Trojan Sexual Health Report Card

100 colleges or universities were selected to be included in the survey, with every state represented by at least one school. The schools were chosen for their size and general level of familiarity to the public. This survey represents 23 percent of total four-year undergraduate college students in the United States

and is representative of the college population. Information was gathered over the course of three months—February to May 2006. Each school received a score of 1–10 in each of seven criteria, and then each of the numeric scores was then converted into a letter grade, from which a score was calculated for each, in the same manner a student's grade point average is computed. Criteria included: Informative and helpful Web site; condom advice and availability; contraception advice and availability; HIV [and] STD testing; sexual assault counseling and services; advice column or Q&A feature for sexual issues or relationships; counseling services, peer counseling, campus events, and other outreach. In the event of a tie, these were decided by comparing the grades in the individual categories, and the schools with the lowest grade or grades that lose to the school with the same score. For example, a school with a C as a lowest of the seven grades would rank above a school with a D or F in one of its categories. In the event of a further tie, the winner was determined by the best score in its Web site. If Web site scores were identical, the winner was the school with the smaller enrollment, with the idea that the smaller school achieves the same results with fewer resources.

| *"Hesitation to talk [about sex] translates into an overall naïveté about the real consequences of sexual relations."*

Students Need to Take Responsibility for Their Sexual Health

Caitlin Myers

Caitlin Myers, Southern Methodist University (SMU) class of 2009, was involved with the college's two newspapers, as a contributing writer to the Daily Campus *and the managing editor of the* Daily Mustang. *The following viewpoint appeared after the campus Web page that disseminated information about sex changed its name from "Women's Health" to "Sexual Health" to emphasize that all students—male and female—have to take responsibility for their sexual behavior. Myers asserts that many students at SMU are not comfortable talking with partners about safe sex and thus do not acknowledge the consequences of unprotected sex. She suggests that part of the problem is that Southern Methodist is a religious school, a circumstance that inhibits students and staff from openly discussing sex.*

Caitlin Myers, "Sex, STIs and Responsibility," *Daily Campus*, April 16, 2008. Reproduced by permission.

As you read, consider the following questions:

1. According to Myers, what percentage of undergraduates surveyed said that both partners should take responsibility for sexual health?
2. How widespread are sexually transmitted infections among Americans, as reported by Myers?
3. How responsible about sexual health and safety do the students at SMU perceive themselves to be, according to the author?

It's two in the morning, and Christine is cold. She walks into a Dallas 24-hour CVS [drugstore], her heels clicking against the linoleum floor. She goes back to the pharmacy area, grabs a purple box of "Her Pleasure" Trojans [condoms] and heads to the checkout. She adds a small bag of Cheetos at the last minute.

"You'll never believe what I just had to do," the 19-year-old business major said once back inside her car and on her cell phone, fuming to her best friend. "My boyfriend just made me go buy condoms."

Students at SMU [Southern Methodist University] have sex. It's a fact. In dorm rooms, cars, Greek houses and apartments. There are the legendary tales of liaisons in Fondren Library and rumors about the front steps of Dallas Hall. There's no denying it; students know a lot about "doing it."

But while sex may be popular, Christine and the other students interviewed for this [viewpoint] refused to speak about it without a promise of anonymity. Their reasons included fear of sorority repercussions, a clash with religious views and a belief that sex is a personal topic. In lieu of their full names, middle names, ages and majors have been used to identify them.

SMU health educator Megan Knapp says this hesitation to talk translates into an overall naïveté about the real consequences of sexual relations—something that SMU is looking to address with more accessible, relatable sexual education efforts.

"I think we create a naïve group of men and women if we're not training them and letting them know what the risks are," Knapp said. "It's real, it's here, it's now. It's not in some, for lack of a better term, whorehouse in Dallas."

Everyone's Responsibility

But despite years of drilling some form of sexual education down Generation Y's throats, be it pro-abstinence programs or safe-sex seminars, one key component seems to have been lost in the shuffle. Who is supposed to take responsibility for staying safe—the man or the woman? And in college, how do students learn about safe sex? How do they communicate with one another about it?

Up until recently, the university's Memorial Health Center Web site led students to believe that sex is a woman's issue. The site listed all information related to sexual intercourse under the "Women's Health" link. Facts on Herpes, HIV, chlamydia and gonorrhea—all sexually transmitted infections (STIs) contracted and transmitted by women and men—were couched on the site titled for females.

"I am shocked to know this," Knapp said upon learning of the Web site's title. "I mean, women are more likely to contract STIs just because of their anatomy, but there's no reason it should be just a women's issue."

The health center, when notified of the discrepancy, changed the link on its main page from "Women's Health" to "Sexual Health."

An online survey of 156 sexually active undergraduates shows that an overwhelming 96 percent believe both partners should take responsibility for staying safe, including avoiding STIs and impregnation.

Why did Christine go to CVS alone?

Most Students Do Not Take Advantage of Health Clinics and other Campus Services

	Evaluation		
Service	Do Not Know (%)	Poor (%)	Aver/Good (%)
Chaplains Office	95.4	1.4	1.9
Counseling Services	89.3	1.4	7.8
Harassment/ Discrimination Office	96.4	1.0	1.2
Health and Safety Office	90.3	1.0	7.1
Health Services	69.9	1.4	27.4
Registered Dietitian	95.4	1.0	2.1
Registrar Services	56.1	4.6	38.3
Security Services	78.4	1.4	18.7
Special Needs Office	90.0	1.0	7.5
Student Health and Development Center	94.4	0.7	3.4
Student Services	66.7	0.0	30.3
Women's Center	94.2	1.7	2.6
Writing Center	88.1	0.5	10.2

TAKEN FROM: Paula Fletcher et al., "Health Issues and Service Utilization of University Students," *College Student Journal*, June 2007.

"Basically, my boyfriend didn't care," she said. "He'd tell me if we're having sex, it's my responsibility to be on birth control and my responsibility to get the condoms."

Where Students Learn About Sexual Responsibility

James, a junior engineering major, says although he used to be "pretty lax" about sexual precautions, he now believes "if you're not taking responsibility, you can't expect someone else to."

And, yet, he says his typical sexual encounter goes something like this:

"If a girl lets you start having sex with her, she's usually on the pill. Like when we're in the middle, I'll ask if she's on the pill, and if she says she's not, I'm like 'What's wrong with you?' And then I'll go and put a condom on or something."

The 20-year-old says he picked up on the negative repercussions of unprotected sex after talking with some guy friends, rather than through sexual education provided by the university.

"We realized that if you get an STD, the next time you hook up with a girl, before you do anything you have to be like, 'Oh, by the way, I have gonorrhea,' and you know she'd be like, 'Umm, we're not hooking up anymore.' So, I'm trying to get more into wearing condoms."

Students at other colleges learn such lessons through the institution they pay to educate them. Take the University of Texas [UT] at Austin. Its student health site contains a page dedicated solely to sexual health with categories including women's health, men's health, sex tips and birth control methods.

"Our site is great because it allows students to get reliable and credible sexual health information whenever and wherever they are," Sandi Cleveland, manager of UT's Health Promotion Resource Center said in a telephone interview.

Cleveland says after the university updated its Web site to include a wider range of educational resources, visitors jumped from 20,000 per month to the current 60,000 to 70,000. . . .

Head a mere 200 miles north, and such candor isn't the norm. With a religious foundation, SMU does not speak as liberally about [sexual] matters. . . .

"I was on the phone with another school's health educator the other day and he was telling me they do courses on how to increase your sexual pleasure," health educator Knapp said. "Could you see that going over here at SMU? No. We do have a conservative campus and as a result I think sexual education does get a little hidden."

Knapp, who started working for the university last summer, says she plans on developing a health site based on peer education where students can request specific sexual health information at their convenience. She says the department has been thinking of updating the Web site for some time but "just hasn't gotten around to it."

Making up for the lack of information on the university's Web site is the controversial gossip site JuicyCampus.com. It provides students with the anonymity they desire when speaking about sexual relations.

One presumably male contributor, calling himself "The Wondering SMU Gigolo," spoke his mind in the following excerpt from his Feb. 24 [2008] post entitled "Sex Without a Condom":

> Having sex w/o a condom feels fantastic. . . . I love it

> But lately, every girl I sleep with has said I dont need a condom. (5 this school year)

> At first I was was like hell yea . . . but now. . . .

> Im thinking girls need to start asking guys to wrap it up. I haven't caught anything I just think I want to be able to sleep with my wife down the line w/o a condom and not catch something from my loved one. all these girls not requiring condoms is going to spread the gross stuff.

The post had been viewed 1,090 times by April 1. Over the same period, the Health Center's Web site was viewed 421 times.

The Consequences of Irresponsibility

The "Wondering Male Gigolo" has a point. Sexual intercourse without a condom helps create startling statistics like these:

One-third of patients in Dallas County infected with STIs are under the age of 25; one in five Americans currently has an STI; more than 80 percent of sexually active college students in the United States will contract some form of HPV [human papillomavirus] before they graduate.

More than half of SMU respondents to the online survey said they had never been tested for an STI before. Of the ones who had been tested, 48 percent said they don't get tested between partners.

In defense of his decision not to get tested, one 21-year-old male survey respondent had this to say: "I have asked three different doctors [about STI testing] and they ask me, 'For what?' And they all say they never test unless the guy has symptoms of an STD."

Health educator Knapp says this couldn't be farther from the truth. Many STIs are asymptomatic, meaning men or women may never see physical signs until it's too late. An untreated STI can lead to pelvic inflammatory disease, cervical and testicular cancer, sterility, ectopic pregnancy, birth defects and death.

"Of course if your partner has a gaping herpes sore you're going to know they have an STI," Knapp said. "But that's the problem—most of the time you'll never know if they have something unless you both talk about it beforehand."

She adds that the only foolproof safe sex is no sex, but if students choose to be sexually active "you should always use protection."

The online survey reveals that, for the most part, male and female students believe they are being responsible when it comes to sex. Nearly all participants reported utilizing at least one of the following: condoms, birth control methods like the pill or a diaphragm and the "pull out" early technique.

It took 20-year-old Rachel five years and more than 10 partners to learn the real meaning of sexual responsibility. The junior advertising major said she was once accused of having an STI when she asked her partner to wear a condom. "From then on, I felt bad for even asking a guy for fear of making it seem like I was the one with a problem," she said.

She has since had two serious relationships, both with guys who "more than willingly" offered to wear condoms. "It wasn't even a question to them; they just automatically got a condom, and I know it sounds stupid, but it made me feel like they really cared about me. It made those two relationships that much better."

For the now-single Christine, she, too, has had to learn this lesson in respect the hard way. Nearing the end of her freshman year, the not-so-naïve coed has had a lot of firsts this year—college parties, final exams, sex and a pregnancy scare.

"I have to take a pill every single day at the exact same time just out of respect for myself and for him," she said. "I don't want to have a kid; I don't want STDs. Why couldn't he [my ex-boyfriend] just grow up and run a five-minute errand to the store?"

> "About 80 percent of college students aged 18 through 23—nearly 7.0 million individuals—were insured through private or public sources of health insurance in 2006."

Most College Students Have Adequate Health Insurance

John E. Dicken

John E. Dicken is the health care director of the United States Government Accountability Office (GAO), an independent, nonpartisan agency that works for the U.S. Congress to investigate how the federal government spends taxpayer dollars. The following viewpoint is excerpted from the GAO's report about health care insurance among college students. It found that about 80 percent of college students do have coverage—mostly through their parents' employer-provided health care plans—and that colleges and state governments are increasingly committed to providing plans designed specifically for this demographic. Furthermore, government legislation also protects students' rights to purchase individual insurance plans.

John E. Dicken, *Health Insurance: Most College Students Are Covered Through Employee-Sponsored Plans, and Some Colleges and States Are Taking Steps to Increase Coverage*, Washington, DC: United States Government Accountability Office, 2008.

As you read, consider the following questions:

1. According to Dicken, what percentage of colleges are estimated to offer student health insurance plans?

2. How does COBRA help college students who become ineligible for coverage on their parents' health care plans, according to the author?

3. What standards for student health insurance programs does Dicken say the American College Health Association has suggested to colleges offering such plans?

About 80 percent of college students aged 18 through 23— nearly 7.0 million individuals—were insured through private or public sources of health insurance in 2006. According to our analysis of CPS [Current Population Survey] data, most college students aged 18 through 23 (67 percent) obtained their health insurance coverage in 2006 through employer-sponsored plans, which are private insurance plans employers offer to employees and their dependents; some (7 percent) obtained coverage through other private health insurance plans, such as student insurance plans offered by colleges; and others (6 percent) obtained coverage through public health insurance programs, such as Medicaid. Of those college students with any form of health insurance in 2006, most obtained coverage through another person's policy, for example, as a dependent on a parent's policy. CPS data also show that 20 percent of college students aged 18 through 23—about 1.7 million students—lacked health insurance in 2006.

Of the 1.7 million college students aged 18 through 23 who were uninsured in 2006, certain groups of students were more likely than others to be uninsured; and uninsured students incurred from $120 million to $255 million in uncompensated care for noninjury-related medical events in 2005. Based on our analysis of CPS data, we found that certain groups of students, including part-time students, older students, students from racial and ethnic minority groups, and students from families with lower incomes, were more likely than other groups of college students to be uninsured. The characteristics of uninsured college students are consistent with those of the uninsured found in the general U.S. population. Our analysis of MEPS [Medical Expenditure Panel Survey] data shows that most of the $120 million to $255 million in uncompensated care costs for noninjury-related medical events incurred by uninsured college students in 2005 was for visits to office-based providers and hospital emergency rooms.

Colleges Support Student Health Care

Over half of colleges nationwide offered student insurance plans in the 2007–2008 academic year and benefits varied across plans. Specifically, we estimate that about 57 percent of colleges nationwide offered health insurance plans to their students, and some types of colleges were more likely than others to offer plans. For example, we estimate that 82 percent of 4-year public colleges nationwide offered student insurance plans in the 2007–2008 academic year, compared with 71 percent of 4-year private nonprofit colleges and 29 percent of 2-year public colleges. Colleges that offered plans varied in the extent to which they made their plans available to part-time students. In general, the plans colleges offered were customized to reflect colleges' priorities in making health insurance premiums affordable for their students while at the same time providing coverage that meets the needs of students. The plans GAO [Government Accountability Office] reviewed varied in the services they covered and how they paid for covered services. Specifically, plans varied in the extent to which they covered preventive services, and some plans set a maximum amount the plan would pay for a particular service. In addition, we found that student insurance plans' annual premiums and maximum benefits varied widely. Specifically, some plans we reviewed had annual premiums that ranged from about $30 to about $2,400, and offered maximum benefits ranging

Percentage of Uninsured College Students, Divided by Race

20 percent of all college students 18–23 were uninsured in 2006

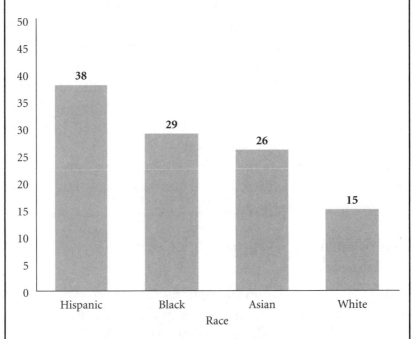

Notes: Only non-Hispanics were included in the black, Asian, and white categories. Differences in the estimates are statistically significant. Estimates for black, white, and all college students are subject to a sampling error within plus or minus 5 percentage points. Estimates for Hispanic and Asian are subject to a sampling error of plus or minus 6 and 7 percentage points, respectively.

TAKEN FROM: Government Accountability Office, *Health Insurance*, March 2008.

from $2,500 for each illness or injury to unlimited lifetime coverage.

Colleges and states have taken a variety of steps to increase the number of insured college students. For example, some colleges have required college students to have health insurance. We estimate that about 30 percent of colleges nationwide required their students to have health insurance for the 2007–2008 academic year. Some states, such as Massachusetts and New Jersey, have also implemented health insurance requirements for college students. In another effort, colleges have jointly purchased health insurance to increase the availability of health insurance for college students and the number of students who are insured. Finally, some states have expanded dependents' eligibility for private health insurance plans, which have traditionally provided coverage for dependents through age 18 and have generally continued coverage for dependents through age 22 only if they attend college full-time. Because most college students obtain health insurance as dependents, these efforts have made health insurance more available to college students. . . .

Health Insurance Options for College Students

College students have several options for obtaining health insurance. They may obtain private health insurance through group market plans offered by employers, colleges, and other groups or through individual market plans. In addition, some college students may obtain coverage through public health insurance programs, such as Medicaid or the State Children's Health Insurance Program (SCHIP).

College students may obtain health insurance through employer-sponsored group market plans, which are plans employers offer to their employees and their dependents. Under these plans, employers typically subsidize a share of employees' premiums for health insurance, and premiums are calculated based on the risk characteristics of the entire group. To offer health insurance, employers either purchase coverage from an insurance carrier or fund their own plans. All plans purchased from insurance carriers must meet state requirements, which vary by state. For example, some states require employer-sponsored plans purchased from insurance carriers to offer coverage to dependents. Although requirements for dependent coverage vary by state, plans have traditionally offered health insurance coverage for dependents through age 18, and have generally continued coverage for dependents through age 22 only if they attend college full-time.

Under federal law, college students who have lost eligibility for dependent coverage under a parent's employer-sponsored insurance plan may be able to use provisions in COBRA [Consolidated Omnibus Budget Reconciliation Act of 1985] to continue their health insurance for a limited period of time. Specifically, COBRA allows individuals such as college students who have lost eligibility for dependent coverage the option of purchasing up to 36 months of continuation coverage under the employer-sponsored plan. COBRA does not require employers to pay for or subsidize this continuation coverage, which can appear expensive in contrast to the subsidized premiums that employees and their dependents may be accustomed to paying for employer-sponsored coverage. COBRA permits employers to charge 100 percent of the premium, plus an additional 2 percent administrative fee.

College students may obtain health insurance through health insurance plans offered by other groups such as their college. Colleges offer health insurance plans to students because they have an interest in maintaining the health of their students and helping them achieve their educational objectives. These plans also can help students avoid high medical bills. To offer a health insurance plan, colleges either contract with an insurance carrier or fund their own plans. Unlike enrollees of employer-sponsored plans, those enrolled in student insurance plans typically pay the full premium for coverage. To make decisions about the plan's eligibility criteria, benefits, and premiums, colleges typically convene a student health insurance committee, which generally includes college administrators, student health center administrators, and student representatives. These committees decide how the student insurance plan will coordinate with a college's student health center, if one exists. College student health centers vary greatly in the services they provide—some offer limited services from one nurse, and others offer extensive services from multiple specialists. The committees may also consider college student insurance program standards issued by ACHA [American College Health Association]. Among other things, these standards suggest that colleges require students to have health insurance as a condition of enrollment, and that student insurance plans provide an appropriate level of benefits, including coverage of preventive services and mental health services and coverage for catastrophic illnesses or injuries.

Health Care Options for Individuals

College students may also obtain health insurance through individual market plans, which are plans sold by insurance carriers to individuals who do not receive coverage through an employer, college, or other group. Because these plans are offered by insurance carriers, the plans must meet state requirements, including those regarding eligibility for dependent coverage. Individuals purchasing a health insurance plan in the individual market typically pay the full cost of their health care premium. Insurance carriers who sell plans in the individual market are typically allowed to review the health status of each individual applying for insurance. Unlike the employer-sponsored group market where premiums are based on the risk characteristics of the entire group, premiums for individual market coverage are based on factors associated with differences in each applicant's expected health care costs, such as health status, age, and gender. Furthermore, applicants for individual market coverage may be rejected.

Some college students may be able to obtain health insurance in the individual market as a result of protections established by HIPAA [Health Insurance Portability and Accountability Act]. Specifically, HIPAA protects eligible individuals, including college students who have exhausted COBRA continuation coverage, by requiring insurance carriers to offer individual market plans without a waiting period for coverage of preexisting conditions. HIPAA also protects eligible college students who were previously and continuously covered by a group market plan and are seeking coverage under a different group market plan. For these individuals, HIPAA requires insurance carriers to limit the use of waiting periods for coverage of preexisting conditions to no more than 12 months.

In addition to private sources of health insurance, college students may obtain health insurance coverage through public health insurance programs, such as Medicaid or SCHIP. Some college students may have coverage through Medicaid, a joint federal-state program that finances health care coverage for certain low-income families, children, pregnant women, and individuals who are aged or disabled. Federal law requires states to extend Medicaid eligibility to children aged 6 through 18 in families with incomes at or below the federal poverty level. Some college students may have coverage through SCHIP, which provides health care coverage to low-income children through age 18 who live in families whose incomes exceed their state's eligibility threshold for Medicaid and who do not have insurance through another source.

> *"College students have become the invisible minority in the national health care debate, as millions— middle-income and students of color especially—go without coverage."*

College Students Are Underinsured

Arelis Hernandez

Arelis Hernandez is a reporter for Diverse: Issues in Higher Education, *a newsmagazine that focuses on matters of access and opportunity in higher education. She has also worked as an intern at Associated Press. The following viewpoint addresses a specific demographic of the American uninsured: college students. Hernandez argues that although recent government reports present traditional college students as a relatively privileged group covered by their parents' health plans and campus services, these people are only a small portion of all students in college. Older adults and minority students from less financially secure families are disproportionately without coverage.*

Arelis Hernandez, "College Students Are Health Care's Invisible Minority," *Diverse: Issues in Higher Education*, September 17, 2009. Copyright © 2009 Diverse: Issues in Higher Education, a CMA publication. Reproduced by permission.

As you read, consider the following questions:

1. How did the Government Accountability Office report overlook so many uninsured college students, according to Hernandez?

2. What kinds of coverage does Hernandez say is often excluded from health insurance plans designed for college students?

3. How does graduation affect a college student's access to health care, according to the author?

Susana Sagastizado, a senior at the University of Maryland, started coughing today. Her nose is running a bit and she feels an ill warmth on her forehead—all bad signs, she said since she doesn't have health insurance.

Luckily, the university's health center provides care at a reasonable price, so Sagastizado can be seen and pay for a flu shot using her part-time income. But if she does have the flu, joining the more than 600 suspected cases at Maryland, it gets worse. The 21-year-old's good fortune could end.

"I worry about it a lot, it's always in the back of my head," Sagastizado said about not having insurance. Her parents can't afford to have her and her two brothers on their insurance without losing their home. "I feel anxious especially when I'm sick. You always think of the worst-case scenario that you might have to go to an emergency room."

College students have become the invisible minority in the national health care debate, as millions—middle-income and students of color especially—go without coverage. On the heels of President Barack Obama's health care speech to students at Maryland [on September 17, 2009], experts interviewed by *Diverse* say college students are being left out.

Rates of Student Coverage Are Overreported

Though often considered the most vibrant and healthy class of privileged Americans, postsecondary students have serious short- and long-term health and financial issues, according to a June 2009 report by a group of college health professionals.

"College students have a higher propensity to be uninsured for longer than other young adults," said Stephen Beckley, a student health insurance consultant for more than 200 schools including Dartmouth College and Duke University. "They use an impressive amount of health care, not unlike other groups."

Beckley is one of the researchers in the Lookout Mountain Group (LMG) report released by an unaffiliated, nonpartisan, grassroots coalition of college health professionals.

Jim Mitchell, the director of the student health services at Montana State University, said when he read Sen. Max Baucus's (D-Mont.) health care bill from the Senate Finance Committee Wednesday [September 16, 2009], he was disappointed.

"They are assuming college students and young adults are the same and they think the solutions they are coming up with for people under 30 will also work for college students," Mitchell said, who helped author that report and has contributed to the American College Health Association [ACHA]. "They are a unique population and they need to be looked at as an individual group."

While in college, many students have health insurance as dependents on their parents' insurance or through a school or private insurer, but many students are falling into a widening chasm in the coverage pool.

Chances are part-time students, minorities, older adults or students at two-year institutions fall among the 20 percent or more than 1.7 million without coverage, according to estimates from a 2008 report to the Senate from the Government Accountability Office [GAO].

But Beckley considers the government's findings misleading because they use a national sample that masks the reality of the uninsured and underinsured in individual states.

The GAO only measured college students between 18 and 23, while Beckley said a growing number of today's students are older than 24, going to school later after working full-time or the military for example. The number of uninsured college students, he said, is somewhere between 4 million and 5 million.

In its annual almanac, *The Chronicle of Higher Education* said since 1980, college students have been getting older and they now consist of 40 percent of all students.

The Limitations of College Plans

The GAO also found that 22 percent of public four-year universities and colleges and 62 percent of private four-year institutions require health insurance as a condition for enrollment for full-time students.

The LMG report estimated that among the insured, between 20 to 30 percent are underinsured or lack adequate coverage.

"Some school-sponsored plans are so nominal in scope of coverage that it's like not having coverage," Beckley said. "The populations they are covering are underinsured and the plans are far from complying with ACHA standards of good insurance."

Some plans even exclude coverage for pregnancy and mental health conditions, and provide poor prescription drug coverage for students who may have chronic conditions, the report said. College students tend to be active, Mitchell said, and most often report accidental injuries.

"Let's say they get a concussion playing sports and end up in the emergency room getting a CAT scan, an MRI, or more," he said. "That can go as far as $3,000 to $5,000 in medical bills."

The ACHA, an advocacy and leadership organization for college and university health, has set standards for health insurance and care for its more than 900 member schools and 3,000 college health care professionals since 1920.

Mitchell, who has contributed to research for the organization, said both he and ACHA support a national mandate for college students to have health insurance but there is no accountability measure in place to make sure health insurance limits are reasonable and affordable.

Even for students on dependent employer-sponsored plans, cost shifting and changes in eligibility requirements place severe coverage restrictions.

Populations Especially at Risk

College students of color have a higher propensity to be uninsured, so coverage can be more a luxury than a necessity since many can't afford it. Disruptions in access make these individuals like Sagastizado vulnerable to high costs and high health risks particularly during flu season.

Sagastizado isn't a typical student. She takes 15 credit hours and works 16 hours a week to help her immigrant parents pay bills. She recently applied for Medicaid, but the history and criminal justice major doesn't think she will be accepted for coverage.

Beckley said his studies have shown that students who are uninsured are twice as likely to have trouble accessing health care later in life, preventing them from receiving preventive care for chronic conditions.

Nationally, minorities are disproportionately represented among the uninsured for young adults between the ages of 19 to 29, according to the Commonwealth Fund, a private organization providing independent health care research.

"There is an existing health system designed for students with nurses, doctors, pharmacies, etc., on college campuses," Mitchell said, "so the kind of insurance they need has to wrap around that system, cover hospitalization cost, and any other catastrophic health issues."

With college graduates coming into one of the worst job markets in 25 years, according to the U.S. Department of Labor—15 percent of 20–24-year-olds were unemployed in June [2009]—the young, dropped and jobless make up at least 30 percent of the uninsured nationwide.

The *Wall Street Journal* reported that recession-era graduates can expect to earn less in wages, trading low-skilled jobs for their dream careers and limiting their health care access.

The [Commonwealth] Fund's 2009 report noted a breakdown in health coverage once a student earns a college degree. A few insurance plans will cover students until their 22nd birthday and some have extended that grace period for recent graduates.

"This is a time when we want them [young adults] to establish connections to the health care system," said Sara Collins, vice president of the [Commonwealth] Fund's Affordable Health Insurance program. Lower incomes will only exacerbate concerns for the fastest-growing segments of the U.S. population without health insurance.

"The pendulum swings between the high expectations of families that the college will 'take care' of 'their babies' and the high expectations of students that privacy rights will be enforced."

Schools Face Dilemmas About Privacy and Intervention When Confronted with Troubled Students

Michael Bogdanoff

Michael Bogdanoff is a litigation attorney with an interest in higher education law. The following viewpoint appeared in the Legal Intelligencer, a daily publication that reports on industry trends, court decisions and verdicts, and law practice issues. Bogdanoff explores the level of responsibility (and legal culpability) universities have toward students who are suicidal, addressing whether they should support the distressed student or instead protect other students who could be harmed by a mental collapse or violent outbreak. He also examines whether a school should involve parents in the health problems of students who are legal adults and protected by privacy laws.

As you read, consider the following questions:

1. According to Bogdanoff, to what did the "special relationship" between the Massachusetts Institute of Technology and Elizabeth Shin give rise?

2. How did the Iowa Supreme Court decide regarding a college's obligation to students in mental distress, as reported by Bogdanoff?

3. What advice does Bogdanoff give to universities about deciding when and how to intervene with troubled students?

Jane Doe was a 19-year-old sophomore enrolled at Hunter College in New York City. She suffered with depression and the pressures of college life. One day, she decided to ingest handfuls of Tylenol in an attempt to commit suicide. This was not Jane Doe's first suicidal gesture. Ironically, Jane also decided to pick up the phone and dial 911. In doing so, she saved her own life.

When she arrived back at the dorms, Jane found that the locks had been changed. Jane checked with her resident director and was told that she had been expelled from the dorms for the semester due to a violation of the campus housing code.

Several months later, Jane found herself arguing to a judge that she suffered from a disability, which entitled her to the rights and protections of the Americans with Disabilities Act (ADA) and Fair Housing statutes. Jane alleged discrimination. She maintained that, in her most vulnerable hour, the college decided to lock her out rather than find her help.

Hunter argued that its housing code was both legal and practical. The code provided that students could not remain in college housing so long as the individual posed an imminent risk to herself or others in the college community. The code also provided for a leave of absence, whereby troubled students would take some time away from the campus, get the help needed, and apply for readmission to housing at a later date.

In September 2006, the judge ruled in favor of allowing Jane's case to proceed. He explained his decision by finding that Jane's display of suicidal behavior could have rendered her "disabled" under the ADA. As a result, reasonable accommodations were necessary. In essence, the judge found that the college may have had the duty to design a plan for Jane to remain part of the college community. The fact that Jane lived on campus made her case even stronger. While not classifying Jane's housing as a custodial relationship, the judge still allowed for the possibility that Hunter took on a heightened duty when hosting residents on its campus.

The Legal Culpability of Colleges

The Hunter College case is just one of a growing number of cases in which students are attempting to impose liability on colleges and universities for failing to address suicidal attempts or gestures in a reasonable and meaningful way. One of the most widely publicized of these cases is that of Elizabeth Shin, the 19-year-old sophomore who allegedly took her life while in her dorm room at MIT [Massachusetts Institute of Technology]. Though Shin had talked of suicide for months and was even hospitalized for a time, the university had allegedly failed to put a comprehensive plan into effect, which would have prevented (or at least mitigated against) Shin's actions.

In allowing the case to go forward, the court was especially concerned with the fact that deans and psychiatrists had a meeting just before the alleged suicide attempt, but put no real plan into effect to address the growing threat. The court found that a special relationship may well have existed between Shin and MIT, giving rise to a heightened duty to protect her from foreseeable harm.

These cases suggest that colleges are in a no-win situation. The college could offer support, but what if it is not good enough for the courts? What if the suicide is completed nonetheless? When do we get the parents involved? Do we not have the right to draft a housing code that protects students against the threat of suicide? Isn't there a time when a leave of absence is appropriate? After a suicidal gesture or attempt, isn't it fair to require students to show that they are not in jeopardy of hurting themselves or others before they are allowed to return to the community? What have we learned from the developing case law and commentary on this issue that can help us plan better, giving students what they need to remain members of the college community while not exposing the college to unnecessary litigation?

The legal and policy issues are many. As a start, we need to understand that the court decisions are mixed on these issues. While Shin is well known and the Hunter College case is very recent, there have been a number of decisions where courts have declined to impose a heightened duty on administrators.

In the highest appellate decision issued to date, the Iowa Supreme Court heard arguments that the college staff's knowledge of a student's mental condition or suicidal gestures created a special relationship whereby the college was responsible for protecting the student from possible harm. In rejecting that argument, the court noted that there is no general duty to protect the student from herself.

There is a way to reconcile these lines of cases. Courts have concluded that, as college personnel gain more knowledge of a student's suicidal thoughts or tendencies, the likelihood of finding a special relationship (imposing a heightened duty) will increase.

Is the solution to leave these students to fend for themselves, to send them off campus, or are there other ways to meaningfully deal with this dilemma? As suicidal students force tough calls for administrators, we need to examine how and when colleges must act when confronted with imminent harm.

When Should Colleges Involve Family?

First, we must realize that colleges are not alone. Parents and friends of the student should be a part of the team. There is no simple way to address a student's suicidal threats or ideations. But those who know the student best can be a valuable asset in supporting them while assisting the college to develop a plan for allowing them to remain on campus or, if necessary, taking a voluntary leave of absence necessary to rehabilitate.

While privacy concerns may be raised, educators are reminded that colleges, while once thought of as *in loco parentis* [in place of the parent], have a more limited role in a student's personal life. Instead, colleges can request what many reasonable institutions do, that is, obtain an emergency contact from the student.

In case of emergency, the college is requested to call one or more friends or family of the student to assist in developing a plan. What is an emergency? The definition should be considered broadly. Suicidal gestures and suicidal ideation may well qualify. As human beings, we press the red emergency button in an elevator when we are stuck between floors for a few minutes without knowing exactly how and when the next events will unfold.

Shouldn't we be pushing the button here? How concerned are we about facing liability for being overprotective and potentially saving a life versus going it alone and taking on more risk? Though the brevity of this [viewpoint] prohibits a lengthy FERPA [Family Educational Rights and Privacy Act] and HIPAA [Health Insurance Portability and Accountability Act] analysis, suffice it to say that both have exceptions to the confidentiality provisions in the case of emergency.

Assume a special relationship will always exist. Though we can say that *in loco parentis* is no longer a viable notion on college campuses, "parents, students and the general community still have reasonable expectations, fostered in part by colleges themselves, that reasonable care will be exercised to protect resident students from foreseeable harm."

When and How to Intervene

Get the student help. How do we know the seriousness of the threat? First and foremost, the student should be required to undergo assessment by health care professionals on or off campus to determine the level of intervention necessary to address the behavior. Move quickly on this and make sure to obtain a good assessment of the student's needs. Design a crisis intervention plan with mandatory counseling by utilizing the health care professionals available to you. The substance of these plans can be left to the behavior specialists. Colleges can enforce the plan as a condition of enrollment.

Avoid punitive measures. At the very least, students will perceive mandatory withdrawal or leave of absence policies as discipline when they are feeling like they have come to you for help. Instead, start the process of educating the student on suicide prevention on the first day of freshman orientation, telling the student what the college can do for them in terms of support, emergency situations, resources on and off campus and how colleges may team with people close to the student when the most dire times exist. Involuntary withdrawal should be a last option, when the health care professionals have indicated that imminent harm will likely result otherwise.

Do not take solace in waiver language on a housing contract or in a student's pledge. The office of civil rights has issued decisions that require a college to do more than simply toss out students who exhibit suicidal behaviors. Colleges are rightfully concerned about discriminating against students who may, at least arguably, have a disability.

That said, there are administrators who may well be troubled by the prospect of a Shin experience. Might liability attach for simply acknowledging the problem and working, in a deliberate fashion, toward a resolution? The answer is that, by teaming up with family and friends, by assuming a special relationship does exist, by putting a plan into place immediately with the aid of health professionals and by carrying out the plan as [a] condition of the student's continued housing or matriculation, the chances of students remaining a part of the college community probably go up and the chances of liability probably go down.

The pendulum swings between the high expectations of families that the college will "take care" of "their babies" and the high expectations of students that privacy rights will be enforced and personal decisions will be honored. But when college administrators or staff have knowledge of suicidal behavior and fail to act in a meaningful way, they are just inviting liability.

Though the Shin decision comes from a trial court in Massachusetts, we should not expect the court's reasoning to be disregarded by other courts as students and their families bring new lawsuits over the handling of suicidal gestures, attempts and even completion. Courts are unlikely to make a college the insurer of the student's safety, but the concept of the "special relationship" will not disappear.

This concept may well be applied in analyzing the college's duty to take appropriate action. Reacting to suicidal behavior is as much a risk management issue as any other. There are no easy fix-its. Colleges should consider taking some time to review how well students are being educated on available resources and how well the college has crafted its policy for dealing with knowledge of suicidal behavior.

Periodical Bibliography

The following articles have been selected to supplement the diverse views presented in this chapter.

Nancy Bell et al.   "'It Has Made College Possible for Me': Feedback on the Impact of a University-Based Center for Students in Recovery," *Journal of American College Health*, May–June, 2009.

Marilyn Elias   "Colleges Put out Safety Nets," *USA Today*, April 15, 2008.

Juliana Hanle and   "Despite Resources, STI Testing Rates a Concern," *Yale Daily News*, February 9, 2010.
Rachel Gilmore

David Moltz   "A Different Kind of Pregnant Student," *Inside Higher Ed*, November 25, 2009.

Holly Prestidge and   "Colleges Make It Easier to Avoid the 'Freshman 15,'" *Richmond Times-Dispatch* (Virginia), September 23, 2009.
Zachary Reid

Carolyn Sayre   "A Lifesaving Vaccine for College Freshmen," *New York Times*, February 13, 2009.

Laura Sessions Stepp   "Beyond the Birds and the Bees," *Washington Post*, October 10, 2006.

Angela Townsend   "Sexual Health a Big Deal at Clinics on College Campuses," *Plain Dealer* (Cleveland, OH), September 1, 2009.

David Weigel   "Welcome to the Fun-Free University: The Return of *in loco parentis* Is Killing Student Freedom," *Reason*, October 2004.

Mark Wolfson,   "College Students' Exposure to Secondhand
Thomas P. McCoy, and   Smoke," *Nicotine & Tobacco Research*, August
Erin L. Sutfin   2009.

Chris Yow   "Snead State Considering Tobacco Ban," *Sand Mountain Reporter* (Alabama), June 24, 2010.

CHAPTER 3

Do Campus Athletic Programs Benefit Students?

Chapter Preface

Reggie Bush is a former football player for the University of Southern California (USC). He played for the USC Trojans football team for three seasons and then left school to play professionally for the New Orleans Saints in 2006. In 2007, sports agent Lloyd Lake filed a lawsuit against Bush to reclaim the cost of "improper gifts" he had given Bush and his family to persuade Bush to work with Lake as his agent. (Bush signed onto the Saints with another agency.) This lawsuit prompted an investigation by the National Collegiate Athletic Association, NCAA, into Bush's tenure as a student-athlete at USC regarding his acceptance of external benefits. The investigation later expanded to cover O.J. Mayo, a USC basketball player suspected of similar wrongdoing.

According to NCAA rules, student-athletes are prohibited from accepting "extra benefits" from sports recruiters or other sports-interested parties, such as financial gifts (like cash or co-signing on a loan), clothes, and electronics (like computers and television sets). The NCAA decided to ban USC from playing in football bowl games for two years and took away twenty football scholarships from its program. USC had already condemned and sanctioned its basketball program after Mayo left, and the NCAA added no further consequences for that department.

The NCAA implemented rules about accepting extra benefits and improper gifts to emphasize that college sports were played by *student*-athletes, not professionals. Its mission is "to integrate intercollegiate athletics into higher education so that the educational experience of the student-athlete is paramount," and allowing players to accept lavish gifts from outside parties would overwhelm their academic interests with financial ones. According to this philosophy, college sports and team participation are experiences that enrich a college education, not vice versa. The NCAA also seeks to ensure that competition is safe, equitable, and sportsmanlike, especially between schools of radically different sizes. Large schools tend to have more money to spend in general, and if they were allowed to lure the best athletes to their programs with material incentives, the smaller schools would never be able to compete fairly against them.

Critics of the NCAA, however, argue that the NCAA does not value student-athletes as students at all. The industry of college sports generates billions of dollars for participating schools, television and other media outlets, and the NCAA itself. Licensing, merchandise, and broadcast rights are negotiated behind the scenes while alumni organizations and booster clubs generate ticket sales for sports events and ancillary functions attended by former students and local fans; college athletes are the foundation of this revenue stream. Many student-athletes are given full scholarships and free room and board in exchange for playing for a school's team, but the NCAA— which partially funds and oversees athletic grants at member schools—limits the number of scholarships a school can offer; schools participating at the Division III level (usually the smallest schools) are not allowed to award athletic scholarships at all. As for making "paramount" the "educational experience of the student-athlete," critics point out that grade point averages are lower and dropout rates higher among student-athletes than the general student population, and their opportunities to participate in extracurricular skills that could better prepare them for non-sports careers after college (such as writing for the college newspaper or interning at a company) are limited by their training and practice schedules.

Disbursing actual paychecks to or sharing royalties with student athletes is one proposed solution to lessening the purported exploitation of their time and talent by college athletics departments and the NCAA; reorganizing the NCAA to make college sports less profitable is another. Colleges could also expand their intramural programs and physical education classes to provide more athletic opportunities to students interested in participating in sports in casual or noncompetitive ways, outside of the structure and rules of the NCAA system. The following chapter explores the ways that schools help students balance athletics and education and how the college experience is affected positively and negatively by the culture of sports.

"Colleges that sponsor programs benefit from an expanded pool of potential students, while the students gain much-needed opportunities."

Athletic Programs Enhance the College Experience

Rob Jenkins

Rob Jenkins is an associate professor of English and director of the Writers Institute at Georgia Perimeter College. He is an occasional contributor to the community college column of the Chronicle of Higher Education. *In the following viewpoint, Jenkins argues in favor of athletics programs at community colleges and takes the stance that they bring more to the school—in student and community interest—than they lose in costs. Furthermore, he asserts, student-athletes at community colleges are more successful than their nonathlete peers and graduate with a two-year degree or transfer to a four-year college at almost twice the rate.*

As you read, consider the following questions:

1. According to the author, why are so many community college administrators willing to cut athletics programs?

2. What are the three points of the author's defense of athletics programs at community colleges?

3. What support system does the author describe that contributes to the academic success of student-athletes at community colleges?

The report caught me off guard: a terse item, buried in the back of the sports section, announcing that Calhoun Community College, in Decatur, Alabama, had discontinued its athletics programs. Even though I'd left coaching two years earlier to pursue a second career in academic administration, I still enjoyed keeping up with old rivals. Calhoun had been the opponent in a 1999 regional semifinal that turned out to be my penultimate game as men's head basketball coach at Alabama Southern Community College. In 2000 the Warhawks at Calhoun advanced to the finals of the NJCAA [National Junior College Athletic Association] men's basketball championship. A year later they were defunct.

As the news sunk in, however, I realized I wasn't really all that surprised. In my 18 years as a community college faculty member, basketball coach, athletics director, department chairman, and academic dean, I've learned that athletics programs are always on the table. Inevitably, there are those among the faculty and administration who view them as a luxury, not as a function central to the core mission of the institution. When budgets are tight, as they usually are, and administrators are looking for a little extra cash, their steely-eyed gaze turns naturally toward athletics.

I experienced that firsthand when, as a young assistant coach at Paducah Community College in Kentucky (now West Kentucky Community and Technical College), I found myself out of a job after the institution dropped its highly successful basketball programs for men and women. Why? "We needed the money for other things," the college's president at the time explained.

In Calhoun's case, years of budgetary shortfalls had left Alabama's two-year colleges scrambling for operating funds. Most managed to hold onto their athletics programs, despite the fiscal crisis, but some felt they had no choice but to let them go.

Athletics Programs Bring Students Together

So I was intrigued last year [2005] when I came across an unusual presentation in the American Association of Community Colleges' convention program: "Enrollment Growth Through Athletics," the title read. Enrollment growth? That sounded suspiciously like a good thing, in sharp contrast to the image of the evil athletics program, siphoning resources while adding little value to the educational mission. This I had to hear.

Paul Thein, vice president of student services and institutional development and director of athletics at Feather River College, explained how his small two-year institution in northern California hit on the novel idea of starting a football program—football!—to rejuvenate sagging enrollment and increase student retention. How they accomplished all that I won't go into here. The salient point is that Feather River began with the assumption that athletics are good for a college, not detrimental, and that they help build academic programs rather than detract from them.

My own defense of community college athletics consists of three points: First, in my experience, they really do increase enrollment and retention; second, they enable a college to serve a wider variety of students by including athletes; and finally, they help foster that sense of community without which a community college is, well, just a college.

Thein was especially adamant about the first point during a conversation I had with him following his presentation. "I don't understand colleges that won't fund athletics but will spend thousands of dollars on so-called 'retention programs,'" he told me. "Athletics is a retention program." According to research conducted for the University System of Georgia, the success rate for two-year college students in Georgia—success defined as graduation and/or transfer—is about 36 percent. Although no one appears to keep comparable statistics for athletes, I'd say their success rate is closer to two-thirds, based on anecdotal evidence I've collected over 18 years at four institutions in four different states.

Why Athletes Are So Successful

One reason for the apparent discrepancy between students and student-athletes is motivation. While many students show up on two-year-college campuses without the faintest idea of what they'd like to be doing a year down the road, athletes are usually intent on competing for four years. Since that means they'll have to transfer at some point, they tend to work toward that goal by attempting to accumulate the necessary credit hours. Indeed, athletes must pass at least 12 hours each semester with a minimum 2.0 GPA [grade point average] simply to remain eligible. So as a group they are highly motivated to go to class, do passing work, and remain enrolled—in theory, at least.

In reality, many athletes are no more highly motivated than other students—some less so. But athletes at most two-year colleges have the advantage of a sophisticated and comprehensive support system: coaches who force them to go to class, assistant coaches and tutors who monitor their academic progress, and required study halls and tutoring sessions. Without that support system, many athletes would undoubtedly drop out. With it, they tend not only to stay in school but usually end up moving on.

Another reason two-year colleges ought to sponsor intercollegiate athletics programs is that a fair number of prospective students are athletes. After all, most community colleges support art, music, and theater programs based on the conviction that they are obligated to serve those individuals in their area who might have an interest in the arts. Why wouldn't the same reasoning apply to athletics?

Of course, not all high school athletes in a college's service area are capable of competing at the collegiate level—but many are. Among those who are, some may choose to play elsewhere. But if the local community college has no athletics programs, that choice has already been made for them.

Athletics Tie the College to the Community

There is even some evidence that athletics programs appeal to students who are not actually planning to participate. As a biology professor at a Florida community college recently told me, the college's reputation for fielding competitive teams is one reason students choose it. "Parents know their kids will get a good education when they come here, but athletics is clearly part of the attraction," he explained. "I believe some students who might have gone elsewhere come here because of our success in athletics. It's part of the total package."

Recently I learned that Calhoun has begun reinstating its athletics programs, beginning with men's baseball and women's softball last fall. Calhoun's new president, Marilyn Beck, who has expressed pleasure at the return of athletics to her campus, notes that the teams will have a decidedly different composition. "In the past," she explained, "we might have recruited athletes from hundreds of miles away. Now we're going to focus on those students in our service area who are interested in sports."

Finally, as Roy W. Johnson, chancellor of the Alabama College System, has noted, athletics programs are "one of the ties that bind the college to the community." Johnson has used his position to help two-year colleges like Calhoun find money to rebuild once-proud sports programs that have fallen victim to the budgetary ax over the years. "A community college is a cultural center for the community, and athletics is a big part of that," he says.

In the end, despite the costs, it's clear to me that athletics have a place on two-year-college campuses. Colleges that sponsor programs benefit from an expanded pool of potential students, while the students gain much-needed opportunities, and community members find yet another reason to embrace the school.

That doesn't sound like a luxury to me.

> "At many of America's largest colleges
> and universities, athletics has become
> overemphasized at great financial, aca-
> demic and, arguably, moral costs."

College Athletic Programs Undermine Academics

**Matthew Denhart, Robert Villwock,
and Richard Vedder**

*Richard Vedder is the director for the Center for College Afford-
ability and Productivity (CCAP) and a distinguished professor of
economics at Ohio University. At the time this selection was
published, Robert Villwock was studying business economics, and
Matthew Denhart was studying economics and political science
at Ohio University. Denhart also worked as a research associate
for the CCAP. The following viewpoint is excerpted from their
report,* The Academics Athletics Trade-Off, *in which they assert
that while participation in athletics offers benefits to individual
university students, it also detracts from the university's educational goals. Costs of sports programs are rising faster than revenues, and athletics programs siphon money away from academics and distract student-athletes from their academic pursuits.*

As you read, consider the following questions:

1. According to the authors, how much did athletic spending increase between 2004 and 2006?

2. How many schools with large athletics programs were profitable in 2006, as stated in this viewpoint?

3. What are some of the changes the authors suggest for numerous universities with good reputations in both athletics and academics?

Intercollegiate athletics is a big business and the expenses to sponsor them are significant. Median total expenses at FBS [Division I Football Bowl Subdivision] schools in 2006 were around $35.75 million and median expenditures per athlete were $65,800. Spending is concentrated largely in the sports of football, basketball, and to a lesser extent, ice hockey. Spending on male athletes was nearly double that of their female counterparts in 2006.

Expenditure growth has not been encouraging. Over the short period from 2004 to 2006, total median athletic expenditures increased 15.6 percent and median expenditures per athlete rose 13.75 percent. With generated revenue growing only 8.3 percent over the same period, it is clear that costs are rising faster than new revenues for athletics. Thus, athletics has become more of a burden on institutional resources over this period.

Salaries for coaches and administrators, athlete grants, maintenance, and rent on facilities and travel costs are notably large. Salaries for top football coaches have, in many cases, reached extraordinary levels. Of those schools where data is available, 69 head football coaches at FBS institutions earned more during the 2006–07 year than that university's president. Beyond high salaries paid to coaches, it seems that athletics departments are typically run by large bureaucracies, with median outlays to administrators around $4.7 million annually. Clearly, an athletic arms race is well under way. Expenses have grown wildly, and top coaches are commanding record sala-

Graduation Rates for the "Elite Eight": 2010 Men's Teams in the NCAA Division I Basketball Tournament

School	Overall Student-Athlete (%)	Overall Basketball Student-Athlete (%)	White Basketball Student-Athlete (%)	Black Basketball Student-Athlete (%)
Baylor	77	36	100	29
Butler	86	90	100	75
Duke	97	92	100	89
Kansas State	77	62	100	38
Kentucky	73	31	100	18
Michigan State	80	58	100	44
Tennessee	76	30	0	38
West Virginia	69	44	60	30

TAKEN FROM: Richard E. Lapchick et al., *Keeping Score When It Counts*, 2010.

ries as schools continue to pour money into athletics. This spiraling spending does little to make school "A" more competitive with school "B" because on balance, for every winner there must be a loser. To bring costs under control, real reform is needed.

Athletics' Effects on Academic Programs

Intercollegiate athletics have many positive benefits. Among many things, sport competitions can create a sense of school spirit and solidarity that extends beyond the immediate campus to help connect far-flung alumni back to their alma mater. Furthermore, athletics benefits the student-athletes themselves. They provide an opportunity for athletically gifted students to pursue their greatest passion while helping to instill important values. Among many things, athletics helps teach responsibility, leadership, competitiveness, sportsmanship, teamwork, cooperation and time-management skills. All of these things contribute to more productive workers upon graduation, advancing society. Beyond that, college sports are a staple of American culture and are a wildly popular form of entertainment.

Lots of college students attend universities or small colleges where there is little in the way of serious intercollegiate athletic competition or where such competition is relatively low key and fairly inexpensive to offer. Some of the nation's top schools have very modest or no intercollegiate athletic competition (schools like the University of Chicago, MIT [Massachusetts Institute of Technology], and Cal Tech [California Institute of Technology] come immediately to mind).

Yet it seems that at many of America's largest colleges and universities, athletics has become overemphasized at great financial, academic and, arguably, moral costs. The fundamental mission of any university should be to advance the knowledge of its students and society through instruction and research. Athletics are often a distraction, both to the athletes themselves and the wider institution in meeting these primary goals. While graduation rate data are still somewhat murky, the low graduation rates among athletics, particularly in sports like football and basketball, is alarming, although there is strong evidence that this problem is endemic to the entire academic enterprise. The introduction of the Academic Progress Rate (APR) by the NCAA [National Collegiate Athletic Association] is a positive development that appears to be helping to provide an incentive for coaches and athletes to take academics a bit more seriously. However, there have also been reports of athletes "clustering" in certain academic majors that are less strenuous in order to meet these new standards. If it is the case that certain athletes can only remain eligible for competition by pursuing meaningless academic endeavors, our universities need to reexamine their priorities before granting them admission to an institution of higher education. By admitting substandard students, universities compromise their academic integrity and have negative spill-over effects on the academic mission.

While the major sports of basketball and football have poorer graduation rates, athletes in many minor sports generally perform much better in the classroom. It appears that smaller sports enhance the athletic department's overall graduation rate performance. This creates the incentive to add a greater number of smaller sports even though they may not be a financially sound investment. Overall, on [former NCAA president] Myles Brand's watch, the NCAA has taken some concrete steps to ensure that athletes remain students first. Enforcement of these policies and continued vigilance is necessary in this area.

Sports Do Not Earn Money for Schools

For virtually all colleges, intercollegiate athletics is not a good financial investment. In 2006, only 19 of 119 FBS institutions realized a net profit from athletics, using a liberal definition of the term "profit." As an average for the entire period from 2004 to 2006, only 16 broke even. Instead of making money, the evidence suggests that allocated revenue (largely coming from the wider university budget) has grown. By 2006, this allocated revenue accounted for more than *a quarter* of total athletic revenues. Since expenditures per athlete have grown more rapidly than generated revenues, athletics have become more of a burden, using up scarce university funds. When considering the opportunity cost of such funds, such as spending to build new classrooms, purchase new technologies, or hire quality faculty, this cost is considerable.

Despite this, the current incentive structure encourages increased spending. The current prevailing wisdom is that spending increases athletic performance. So, schools try to buy the best coaches, and spend a lot to buy the best facilities in order to recruit good athletes. In some aggregate sense, this is doomed to failure, since the average of all relevant teams wins 50 percent of its games—for every winner, there is a loser.

Donations from alumni and others are the second highest revenue generator among FBS athletic programs. The effect of athletic success on donations has been the subject of several scholarly studies, and we would conclude that the evidence is inconclusive, with their perhaps impacting less distinguished academic institutions more than schools with an existing reputation for academic excellence. On the whole, the argument that successful athletics is necessary to maximize donations to academics appears somewhat dubious.

With growing expenses in a time of budget shortfalls, reform of athletic expenses is needed. The salaries of coaches and athletic administrators seem out of line with institutional priorities. In 2006, 48 head football coaches made in excess of $1 million and 69 earned more than their university's president. Travel expenses are another large expense. Teams often have to charter flights and stay in hotels for multiple nights to compete in games and tournaments in hard-to-reach locales.

Grants-in-aid are the number two expense for athletics. This expense has grown significantly as college tuition and room/board costs have soared. Over the 30-year period from 1976 to 2006, such costs have increased on average 2.4 percent compounded annually. This has been far greater than both the growth in inflation and personal incomes. It is clear that much reform is necessary beyond athletics to solve these problems.

It is unlikely that universities and/or their athletics cartel, the NCAA, are going to reform spending on their own, and given the popularity of college sports, political leaders are hesitant about forcing changes that might incur the wrath of sports fans. Yet, as financial pressures rise on schools, the ability to effect real reform is growing. What form might reform take? Below we outline a scenario that might be plausible and might work.

Reforming Athletics to Support Academics

Suppose the leaders of 25 to 30 universities, most of them with good athletic reputations as FBS schools and also with relatively high academic reputations, were to get together to call for a radical revision of college athletics. For example, what if schools like the University of Michigan, University of Illinois, University of North Carolina, University of Virginia, Duke University, Stanford University, University of Notre Dame, University of California (Berkeley), University of Washington, University of Texas, Northwestern University, Ohio State University, University of Southern California, Boston College, University of Georgia, UCLA [University of California (Los Angeles)], University of Florida, Wake Forest, Vanderbilt, and the University of Wisconsin gathered, with the support of the eight presidents of the Ivy League schools (Harvard, Yale, Princeton, Columbia, Pennsylvania, Brown, Dartmouth and Cornell)? These schools represent a significant portion of several major athletic conferences, including the Southeastern Conference, Big Ten, Pacific-10, Big 12, and Atlantic Coast Conference, as well as the entire Ivy League.

Suppose these schools say they are going to:

- Reduce the length of seasons, number of games, size of coaching staffs, and the number of permissible players in football and perhaps other sports;

- Play at least 80 percent of their matches with other schools adhering to these reform principles;

- Form at least two new conferences (seriously gutting five major existing conferences in the process);

- Outlaw redshirting [when a student delays sports participation for one year and graduates after five years] and other practices that detract from emphasizing the primacy of academic matters even for athletes;

- Prohibit play during examination periods;

- Put limits on coaches' salaries and put a limit on administrative staff size;

- Insist that athletic departments be under the control of a university official such as the provost;

- Put strict limits on the size of institutional subsidy for the athletic programs;

- Put academic officials in firm control of changes in conference/national association policies (or at least give them a veto power);

- Strictly limit post-season participation in bowl games, etc.

It is an interesting issue whether the university presidents could pull this off and whether alums, legislators, or others would try to derail the reforms, etc. On the other hand, seeing a large number of prestigious and also athletically proficient schools sign on might bring others along for the reforms—Penn State [Pennsylvania State University] might follow the lead of Ohio State, for example, Texas A & M the lead of Texas, and Virginia Tech the lead of Virginia. Obviously, the larger the initial group that agrees to the principles, the greater the probability the effort will succeed.

Long before sports became as commercialized as they are now, huge crowds gathered to watch Harvard play Yale, Michigan play Ohio State, Army take on Navy, etc. School spirit can exist, entertainment can be provided, and athletic programs can be at most a minor financial drain on institutions. An athletic disarmament conference might work, if dominated by academic types and not coaches, athletic directors, and fanatic alums.

"It is precisely the willingness to put up with these uncomfortable . . . antics that indicates you care deeply about membership."

Hazing Rituals Strengthen Teams and Bond Teammates

Gary Alan Fine

Gary Alan Fine is a professor of sociology at Northwestern University. His research interests include social psychology and collective behavior; he is also the author of the book With the Boys: Little League Baseball and Preadolescent Culture. *The following viewpoint was written in response to the suspension of student-athletes at Northwestern University after their participation in the hazing of teammates was exposed to school officials. Fine defends the tradition of hazing as an important group-bonding ritual that creates stronger teams and forges lifelong networks of camaraderie and support.*

As you read, consider the following questions:

1. According to the author, how does participating in hazing rituals encourage bonding among members?

2. According to Fine, how do rules prohibiting hazing contribute to the excessive nature of current hazing practices?

3. Why does Fine argue that hazing is only effective when teammates don't share pictures of it with others?

Hazing is good for America. Those of us who have been through fraternity (and some sorority) initiations, at one time a hallowed part of campus life, know that they develop shared feelings of honor and pride. But such rituals have been toned down in today's no-risk, litigious, surveillance society. Where once we accepted the rough-and-tumble of youth culture, now everything is examined through the thorny eyes of lawyers.

Recently, Northwestern University suspended some members of the women's soccer team from some 2006–07 regular season games for hazing. Some players also received probation and others unspecified "additional disciplinary action." The men's swim team and the Northwestern Wildcat mascot squad also were punished in separate incidents.

The truth is that in almost all instances hazing is not harmful. Girls will be girls (and boys, boys) and any punishment will be ineffective. And hazing rituals have real benefits.

Benefits of Hazing

Initiations require mutual support and bonding among members. The initiates give up some of their dignity, smudge their reputations, because they know that others in the group will have done the same. They gain a confidence that their mates will support them through college and after. Those more senior know that the initiates wish to join with such intensity that they are willing to let themselves be humiliated. You agree to become the butt of a collective joke, shrouded in secrecy. No one will ever know, so one's public self is preserved.

Being told that you're going to eat worms, strip to your skivvies, or chug a few beers while being paddled is not everyone's idea of fun. But it is precisely the willingness to put up with these uncomfortable (and sometimes painful) antics that indicates you care deeply about membership. The group matters. Initiates give up part of their personal reputation to acquire the benefits of the reputation of the team. And this strengthens the group and the person.

Indeed, what is striking about the women's soccer initiation at Northwestern is that all reports suggest the women participated voluntarily and considered it fun.

Hazing Needs Limits

Granted, initiations can go too far. Some rules are essential (no sexual contact, reasonable boundaries on physical punishment, and, most significantly, demands that the organizers refrain from alcohol). Excessive practices often occur when authorities prohibit initiations. When we do not teach teenagers how to drink responsibly, they learn to drink rapidly and to excess. When initiations are pushed underground, they are recreated without tradition and sometimes without boundaries. When universities do not learn that bonding rituals are valid and valuable, they respond with fear and create foolish rules that encourage violations.

Initiations were once tied mostly to the doings of college men. Perhaps the sexist idea that this rough sport was acceptable for boys led to a greater acceptance of these rituals. However, female athletes and sorority members are now quite as wild as their male counterparts. And good for them. Bonding used to be a male activity, but now female bonding serves the same valid purposes as they did for their brothers.

However, one rule should be inviolable. No Internet pictures. Today the tut-tut images of young adults romping in their panties, downing brews, being bound with tape or giving lap dances on Web sites such as Badjocks.com combine smarmy voyeurism with unctuous morality, the worst of both worlds. For hazing to have its positive effects, it must separate the group from those outside to create a powerful connection among members.

College administrators may want to punish students for their violations, but these are rules that no one needs or wants.

Left alone, these students will create connections that will serve them for life. Just ask President [George W.] Bush and Sen. John Kerry (D-Mass.) and their Skull and Bones [a social organization at Yale University] brothers.

| "Students who have reported hazing perceive that the experience allowed them to feel more like a member of the team."

Regardless of Student Perceptions, Hazing Is Dangerous and Harmful

Jennifer J. Waldron

Jennifer J. Waldron is an assistant professor in the School of Health, Physical Education, and Leisure Services at the University of Northern Iowa, where she specializes in the psychosocial aspects of sports. In the following viewpoint, she describes the group-bonding rituals known as hazing. Researchers have found that hazing—which is often banned by school administrators—is popular among sports teams at the high school and college level. She points out that researchers have also found that athletes consider these activities an important part of the group experience and team tradition, and often do not regard them as "hazing" at all. Waldron asserts that hazing rituals are often dangerous and humiliating, and coaches and school administrators should take steps to deter such actions.

Jennifer J. Waldron, "I Have to Do What to Be a Teammate?" *JOPERD—The Journal of Physical Education, Recreation & Dance*, vol. 79, May 2008, p. 4+. Copyright © 2008 American Alliance for Health, Physical Education, Recreation, and Dance. Reproduced by permission.

As you read, consider the following questions:

1. What is the definition of "hazing" that appears in this viewpoint?
2. According to Waldron, how do athletes perceive the behaviors commonly labeled "hazing"?
3. What other group-bonding activities could be implemented in lieu of hazing, according to the author?

Participating in a drinking game, drinking large amounts of alcohol or non-alcoholic beverages, singing or chanting in public, and being screamed at by teammates are examples of hazing events that "rookies"—the new members of a sport team—often experience. Hazing has been defined [by N.C. Hoover] as "any activity expected of someone joining a group that humiliates, degrades, abuses, or endangers, regardless of the person's willingness to participate." Recently, a national study was released reporting the hazing behaviors of college students. In one of the most extensive studies of hazing to date, the researchers received responses from more than 11,500 undergraduate students about their hazing experiences. Additionally, the researchers interviewed 300 students and campus personnel in order to glean a deeper understanding of hazing experiences. The results revealed that seven out of 10 varsity athletes and six out of 10 club-sport athletes reported hazing behaviors. Clearly, hazing is a common experience for college students, particularly athletes, who want to join an organization or team. The purpose of this [viewpoint] is to underscore some of the findings from the report and to highlight what coaches, teachers, and administrators can do to decrease the incidence of hazing.

Student Perceptions of Hazing

Many hazing experiences include risky and dangerous behaviors, such as drinking alcohol, being deprived of sleep, getting a tattoo, and performing sex acts, which may lead to serious health consequences. Furthermore, it is common for the media to report hazing experiences to the public only when someone has been injured or hurt. For example, the incident that occurred at Glenbrook High School in Illinois in 2003 received a great deal of media attention. Junior-class girls were punched and kicked, and had feces, urine, toxic paint, pig intestines, fish guts, and blood thrown on them. The resulting injuries included a cut requiring stitches, a broken ankle, hearing loss, and a bacterial infection due to being force-fed excrement. In spite of these potential consequences, many athletes do not consider hazing to be harmful to themselves or to others.

Many students perceive that hazing results in positive outcomes for the team or the club. When asked, students who have reported hazing perceive that the experience allowed them to feel more like a member of the team or group. Another study found that high school athletes were willing to comply with hazing in order to prove themselves or to be perceived as cool by their teammates. Hazing, then, is perceived to contribute to team cohesion, and by enduring hazing, rookies prove they are committed to the team. This desire to do whatever is required—even if it is risky and dangerous—in order to be a full-fledged member of a team, is a pervasive characteristic of hazing.

Many athletes have such a strong desire to remain a member of a team that they do not realize or want to acknowledge that they are being hazed. While only 12 percent of collegiate athletes reported being hazed, 79 percent of them described behaviors that would be identified as hazing. Additionally, nine out of 10 students who have experienced hazing in college do not consider themselves to have been hazed. Instead, students reported that "it was no big deal," "it was a tradition," and "I was a willing participant." It would seem that many athletes view hazing not as hazing, but as required behaviors to become a full-fledged member of the team. This is a concern for two reasons. First, although rarely invoked, 44 states in the United States have laws deeming hazing illegal. By not considering their activities hazing, many students and athletes often do not realize they are breaking the law. Second, many of the hazing acts are humiliating, brutalizing, and potentially life threatening. When athletes perceive that hazing is a requirement of team membership, they are often putting their life and potentially other people's lives at risk.

Hazing Is Hardly a Secret

Another tacit imperative when participating in hazing is that both hazers and hazees must adhere to the culture of silence. For example, 60 percent of collegiate athletes reported that they would not report being hazed because of the risk of being ostracized. Specifically, many athletes do not speak against the hazing practices for fear of disobeying or challenging the hazers and facing the consequences. Reasons for not reporting hazing activities, cited by 95 percent of students who were hazed, included (1) not wanting to get their team or group in trouble, (2) being afraid of negative consequences including being physically hurt, and (3) being concerned they would become an outsider. Although athletes are expected to remain silent about hazing and not report hazing to officials, this is sometimes contradictory because many hazing practices also have a public aspect to them.

Currently, the public aspect of hazing takes on one of two forms. First, 25 percent of students reported that their hazing experiences occurred in a public space on campus. It is possible that hazing activities occurring in public create a greater "risk" of public humiliation and of being caught by officials. This may make the hazing activity a more valuable assessment of "worthiness" to be a team member. The second public aspect of hazing is the posting of photos and videos on the Web. [E.J.] Allan and [M.] Madden reported that more than

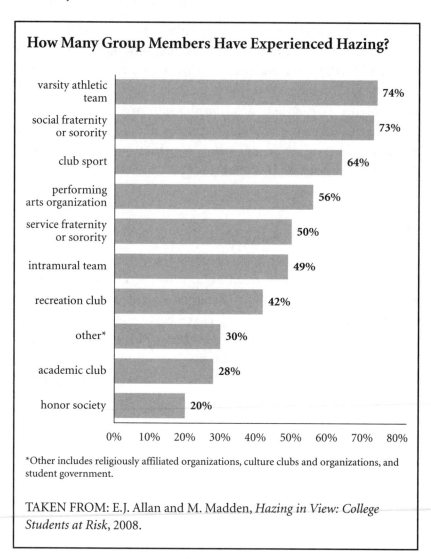

How Many Group Members Have Experienced Hazing?

varsity athletic team	74%
social fraternity or sorority	73%
club sport	64%
performing arts organization	56%
service fraternity or sorority	50%
intramural team	49%
recreation club	42%
other*	30%
academic club	28%
honor society	20%

0% 10% 20% 30% 40% 50% 60% 70% 80%

*Other includes religiously affiliated organizations, culture clubs and organizations, and student government.

TAKEN FROM: E.J. Allan and M. Madden, *Hazing in View: College Students at Risk*, 2008.

50 percent of the students who reported hazing stated that photos of the activities were posted on public Web sites. These photos are often shocking in nature. For example, in 2006, the Northwestern University women's soccer team posted photos from an evening filled with hazing behaviors, including underage drinking, forced exercise, hands tied behind backs, and

sexual acts. It is possible that posting public photos reinforces one's status as a team member by showing others, outside of the team, that the initiate endured the hazing activity. On a positive note, the public posting of hazing photos has allowed staff and administrators to learn about hazing practices occurring at their school.

Deterring Hazing Is Critical

Within the sport environment, teachers, coaches, administrators, and team leaders need to work to deter hazing practices. First, it is important that educational institutions make a commitment to hazing prevention by having a sound policy in place. This policy should be disseminated at the institutional (e.g., college), departmental (e.g., athletic department), and team level. For example, the incident at Northwestern University prompted the athletic department to provide an institutional brochure about hazing to each coach and athlete, who then has to formally acknowledge receipt. Awareness, knowledge, and education are methods that can be used to deter hazing; however, other strategies also need to be implemented.

From the studies, it is apparent that the desire to be a member of the team is a motive for athletes to acquiesce to hazing practices. It will take courage for athletes to report these cases because of the code of silence. Since students have reported that the most beneficial factor in removing themselves from a potential hazing situation was to have supportive friends outside the organization where the hazing was occurring, it is crucial that coaches, administrators, and schools create a safe environment in which athletes feel comfortable and supported to report hazing incidents. For example, athletic departments can create a system to report hazing incidents in a confidential manner. With this approach, athletes would not risk teammates knowing who made the report.

Finally, administrators, teachers, coaches, and team leaders need to promote rituals that generate partnerships within and among teams rather than rituals that generate rivalry and hostility. Both Baylor University and Mothers Against School Hazing have a list of hazing alternatives that can be consulted. These alternatives include establishing a Big/Little Sis or Bro program with older and younger team members and experiencing a ropes course together. It is imperative that schools and colleges are proactive in deterring hazing activities on their campuses. As [a 2008] study has shown, hazing continues to be a problem with students and athletes. It is hoped that the progress already made in curtailing this practice can be continued and expanded in the future.

> "[By 2004] the female share of the college athletics budget had increased to 37% of the operating budget, 45% of the athletic scholarship dollars, and 33% of the recruiting budget."

Title IX Has Improved Sports Programs

Cathryn L. Claussen

Cathryn L. Claussen is the director of the Sport Management program at Washington State University, where she researches civil rights in the context of sports and legal issues of college athletics, and she teaches courses in sports law, sports ethics, and sports sociology. The following viewpoint describes the effects of Title IX, an American law passed in 1972 that requires schools to provide equal access for men and women to all school subjects and to athletics programs. Claussen addresses the controversy that still surrounds the law and explains the benefits that women and women's sports programs have enjoyed in the decades since its implementation.

Cathryn L. Claussen, "Female Sports Participation in America: The Effectiveness of Title IX after 35 Years," *International Sports Law Journal*, 2007, pp. 79–82. Copyright © 2007 ASSER International Sports Law Centre. Reproduced by permission.

As you read, consider the following questions:

1. According to Claussen, on what three aspects of school sports funding does Title IX legislation focus?

2. Why has women's interest in sports participation at college been lower than men's interest in sports participation, in Claussen's view?

3. What long-term personal advantages are associated with high school sports participation as measured by the National Center for Education Statistics?

There are few opportunities for women to participate in sport at the professional level, with the primary exceptions of tennis and golf. In the United States, professional team sport opportunities for women in other sports are struggling. The Women's National Basketball Association (WNBA) has experienced some success, but similar efforts in the sports of softball, boxing, volleyball, American-style football, and soccer have not been as successful. In the U.S., college sports teams typically serve as the training ground for professional sport athletes, so this [viewpoint] is focused on school sport because this is where the majority of participation opportunities for women currently exist. This [viewpoint] examines how effective Title IX, an American law that was passed in 1972 to achieve gender equity in educational settings, has been in promoting the participation of girls and women in sport. . . .

Understanding Title IX

The law itself is a simple one and reads as follows:

> No person in the United States shall, on the basis of sex, be excluded from participation in, be denied the benefits of, or be subjected to discrimination under any education program or activity receiving federal financial assistance.

After its passage, the question remained, how should the concept of prohibiting sex discrimination in education programs be applied to the context of school and college athletics? To flesh this out, the U.S. Department of Education's Office for Civil Rights put forth regulations that provide more specific guidance. These regulations focus on three aspects of school athletics:

- Athletics scholarships

- Participation opportunities

- Other athletics benefits (i.e., provision of equipment and supplies; provision of locker rooms, practice and competitive facilities; publicity; opportunity to receive coaching and academic tutoring; assignment and compensation of coaches and tutors; scheduling of games and practice time; travel and per diem allowance; provision of medical and training facilities and services; provision of housing and dining facilities and services)

Subsequently, in 1979 the Office for Civil Rights issued a policy interpretation that was intended to further clarify how schools and universities could comply with the regulations. This policy interpretation contained a three-part test for compliance on the issue of equitable participation opportunities. A school would be considered to be in compliance with Title IX if it could satisfy any one of the three parts of this test. The three-part test is structured as follows, with an illustration of proper compliance included [after] each of the parts:

1. Substantial proportionality of female athletes to female undergraduate students. [If women are 50% of students, they should be close to 50% of athletes.]

2. History & continuing practice of improving opportunities for females. [If a school added 1 sport for females every 3–5 years within past 15 years, it has made a good faith effort and will be considered in compliance.]

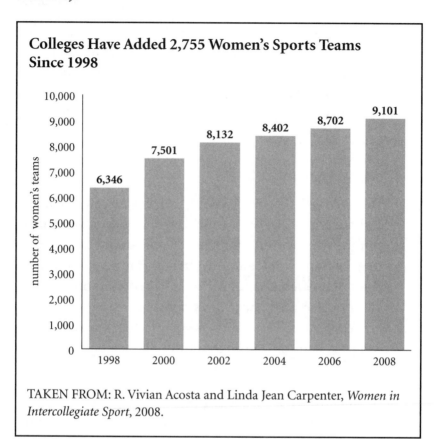

Colleges Have Added 2,755 Women's Sports Teams Since 1998

number of women's teams

	6,346	7,501	8,132	8,402	8,702	9,101
	1998	2000	2002	2004	2006	2008

TAKEN FROM: R. Vivian Acosta and Linda Jean Carpenter, *Women in Intercollegiate Sport*, 2008.

3. Full & effective accommodation of interests & abilities of females. [If there is an existing varsity team, it is best not to eliminate it; if there is an existing club team, a school should consider elevating it to varsity status upon justified request.]

Defending Title IX Against Controversy

This three-part test has generated much controversy, and has been challenged as unfair by male football and wrestling coaches associations and male college athletics directors. They have argued that the first prong of the test is an unfair quota system that constitutes improper affirmative action for females, and has led to existing men's teams being eliminated. But of course, in order to know whether equity has been achieved, there must be some way to measure it. This first part of the test is intended to provide athletics administrators with an objective, measurable way to know if they are complying with the law. It is not a quota system, because if a school cannot meet this safe harbor, the test provides other options for demonstrating compliance with the law. Also, blaming Title IX for the elimination of non-revenue-generating men's sports such as wrestling, gymnastics, and swimming is simply wrong. Title IX does not require athletic departments to eliminate men's teams to bring the participation ratio into substantial proportionality. Athletic departments can find other ways to do so, for example by cutting unnecessary costs and raising new funds. That they have chosen to eliminate minor men's sports teams is simply evidence that universities are prioritizing football over the other men's sports.

If not in compliance as measured by the first prong, a school can always attempt to satisfy the law by demonstrating compliance as measured by the second or third parts of the test. Most of the lawsuits so far have been won by the plaintiffs, and have rested on prong one because most universities could not satisfy the second or third prongs. However, some schools are beginning to show evidence of sufficient improvements in female participation opportunities over time that they can now satisfy prong two.

A big controversy still exists over how to satisfy prong three. Title IX opponents often argue that women are not as interested in participating in athletics as men are, and therefore do not deserve equal participation opportunities. This ignores the reality that a history of discrimination in providing opportunities will depress interest until opportunities have been put in place for a sufficient time for interest to develop. For example, if I had grown up in Africa in the Sahara desert, it is unlikely that I would have a current interest in participating in ice hockey. As another example, young girls have never had the opportunity to participate in tackle football, and so would obviously not have had the chance to develop an interest in playing that sport. Compare these situations with the situation of the relatively recent widespread introduction of youth soccer in America. From the beginning, opportunities were provided for both sexes and now we see both sexes quite interested in participating in soccer. The principle here is that "If you build it, they will come." Opportunity dictates interest but it does take time for interest to develop. . . .

Positive Effects of Title IX

Title IX has contributed to some positive changes in opportunities for girls and women. Prior to the passage of Title IX, women earned very few of the advanced degrees awarded by universities. For example, in 1971, women earned 1% of the dental degrees, 7% of the law degrees, 9% of the medical degrees, and 14% of the doctoral degrees awarded. This is an indication that many professions were not considered viable options for women.

With regard to sport participation opportunities for females prior to Title IX, only 295,000 girls played high school sports compared to 3.7 million boys. That means that only 7.4% of high school athletes were female in 1971, and their sports programs received only 1% of the athletics budget. Females in college sports did not fare much better back then. In 1971, 32,000 women participated in college athletics compared to 180,000 men. Thus, only 15% of college athletes were female, and their programs received only 2% of the athletics operating budget.

The situation is now much different. In terms of advanced degrees awarded to women, in 2003 women earned 39% of dental degrees, 49% of law degrees, 45% of medical degrees, and 47% of doctoral degrees, and virtually any career (with the exceptions of certain military positions and professional sports) is open to women.

With regard to high school and college athletics, in 2004 42% of high school athletes and 43% of college athletes were female; moreover, the female share of the college athletics budget had increased to 37% of the operating budget, 45% of the athletic scholarship dollars, and 33% of the recruiting budget. Particularly impressive is the dramatic increase in numbers of female high school athletes from 295,000 in 1971 to 2.95 million in 2004. Because the opportunities for both males and females are so limited at the college level, this large change at the high school level has been very important in providing competitive sport opportunities for large numbers of females.

Increased sport participation also seems to contribute to a better life for women after their school days are over. One research study conducted by the National Center for Education Statistics followed up on a set of 1992 high school graduates to examine their status in the year 2000, eight years after graduation. 72% of the males and 49% of the females reported having participated in athletics back when they were in high school. Regardless of sex, compared to non-participants those who had participated in high school athletics were more likely to have completed an undergraduate college degree, be earning a higher annual income, and be participating currently in fitness or group sports or recreation activities.

Furthermore, of women in this age cohort, the women that completed high school in the years after Title IX was enacted participated in sports in significantly greater numbers. A 1992 study that compared white-collar working women from the pre–Title IX age generation to those who had attended high school after Title IX was in place found that while 48% of the pre–Title IX age group had participated in youth sport, 64% of those working women from the post–Title IX age group had done so. Similarly, 36% of the pre–Title IX generation had participated in high school sports, whereas 55% of the post–Title IX group had done so.

Additionally, in a 2001 survey of high-level female business executives, a majority of those women credited their past sport participation with helping to develop their business skills, 86% said sport participation helped improve their self-discipline, 81% their teamwork, 69% their leadership skills, and 59% their competitiveness. Of these women, 82% reported participating on organized sports teams after elementary school age, and 81% reported that they were currently participants in sport and/or physical activity. 66% said they exercised at least three times per week—compared to one-third of women in the general American population. 75% said they preferred an athletic body over a thin "model" body. These data, while not capable of describing a causal relationship, do suggest that for women there is some positive correlation between sport participation and later success as a career professional.

Remaining Gender Inequity

In spite of great improvements due at least partly to Title IX, several areas of gender inequity in sport participation remain. While females represent 42% of high school athletes, they are 47% of the high school student body. And while females represent 43% of college athletes, they are 57% of the university undergraduate student body. Additionally, while female college athletes receive a much larger share of the athletics operating budget than in the past (37% compared to 2% in 1971), they still receive less than an equitable share given their proportional representation in the student body. One way of understanding the inequity of this situation is to use a role reversal mental exercise. If male and female participants were to trade places, would the males be happy with what they would then have?

Other continuing concerns include: continuing inequities in numbers of coaches for female teams and inequities in salaries for coaches of women's teams doing comparable jobs as coaches of men's teams; a lack of government support for investigative and enforcement efforts; persistent conflict over the three-part test and the appropriate means for assessing equity; a perception that females are less interested in sports than males; and the almost sacred status of American football. Some people are still calling for football to receive special treatment and not be included as a male sport when trying to balance participation opportunities for males and females. Why this should be so remains unclear unless football players constitute a third sex!

In addition to the inequities that have been consistently observed through the past 30 years, some new problems with the implementation of Title IX have been identified recently. One is that except for cross-country running and indoor track, the sports most frequently added for females in the post–Title IX era tend to be activities in which students from ethnic minority and lower socioeconomic groups are not highly represented. These sports include soccer, softball, golf, lacrosse, rowing, water polo, equestrian, rifle, and ice hockey.

Another is that some of the sports being added for women, such as bowling, equestrian, and rifle, are not activities that promote better physical fitness very well. If fitness is meant to be an important factor in school sports, then this issue should receive consideration in determinations about which sports to add for females in the future.

"Current Title IX enforcement has demeaned the legitimate athletic and academic accomplishments of women and institutionalized discrimination against boys and men in schools."

Title IX Undermines Sports Programs

Allison Kasic and Kimberly Schuld

Allison Kasic is the director of the R. Gaull Silberman Center for Collegiate Studies, and Kimberly Schuld is the former director of gender equity and Title IX projects at the Independent Women's Forum (IWF), an institute that focuses on issues that concern men, women, and families and that advocates personal responsibility and limited government. The following viewpoint is excerpted from IWF's position paper about Title IX. The authors argue that the way the Title IX legislation has been applied constitutes a radical feminist act that has harmed men's and women's collegiate sports programs and has encouraged quotas and discrimination. Title IX, they assert, attempts to treat male and female athletes the same, ignoring differences in interest level and physiology. The inappropriate application of Title IX,

Allison Kasic and Kimberly Schuld, *Title IX and Athletics: A Primer*, Washington, DC: Independent Women's Forum, 2008. Copyright © 2008 Independent Women's Forum. All rights reserved. Reproduced by permission.

the authors conclude, has not only damaged men's collegiate athletics but has also undermined women's sports and inhibited growth.

As you read, consider the following questions:

1. According to the authors, how has Title IX contributed to the discrepancy between the men's and women's cross-country teams at James Madison University?
2. What link do the authors make between a successful college football program and successful women's sports programs?
3. In the authors' view, how does setting high minimums for the number of participants on women's teams undermine the competitiveness of women's athletics?

Title IX long ago ceased to be an effort to guarantee equal opportunities for all, and has instead become a crusade to impose quotas and gender preferences in schools.

At issue is not the Title IX statute itself, which simply outlaws discrimination in educational institutions on the basis of gender. The problem is the way in which Title IX has been applied. Feminists have used Title IX as their all-purpose vehicle to advance a radical agenda in our schools, and have imposed this agenda on a willing bureaucracy and the federal courts. As a result, current Title IX enforcement has demeaned the legitimate athletic and academic accomplishments of women and institutionalized discrimination against boys and men in schools.

Specifically regarding athletics, the Department of Education's policy of compliance through proportional participation rates is the crux of the problem. The government claims that if the percentage of female athletes is close to the percentage of all female students, a school has proved nondiscrimination. If those numbers are not "proportional," schools may be out of compliance with Title IX. In simpler terms, under this view of Title IX, men can play sports only to the extent that women are interested in playing sports.

By demanding that women participate in athletics at the same rate as men, Title IX policy ignores not only legitimate differences between men and women but legitimate differences among women. We are not all athletes, and we are not all scholars. We look to ourselves, not the government, to know the difference.

Title IX policy also undermines equal opportunity by forcing colleges and universities to eliminate men's sports opportunities in order to provide few or no new opportunities for women. This is not fighting discrimination against women; this is enforcing quotas against men. . . .

The Interest-Level Problem: More Men than Women Pursue Athletics

Men and women are not the same; their interest in organized sports is not the same. Title IX should focus on the overall availability of opportunities to accommodate interest, not on the selections of those opportunities by one sex or the other. Ironically, Title IX policy ignores actual interest levels and capabilities of either sex as determining factors in whether the interests and abilities of students have been met.

A variety of research points to lower interest in sports, on a variety of levels, among girls compared to boys. Girls' participation rates and behaviors in all types of physical activity consistently lag behind those of boys. Boys are more likely to participate on sports teams than girls. Girls also join organized sports at later ages than boys and drop out earlier.

Many Title IX advocates say, "If you build it, they will come." But that hasn't proved true. When Brown University was sued in 1992 under Title IX, the varsity female teams at the university had more than 80 unfilled slots. The school had built it, but the women didn't come. Further, coaches of female teams have talked on camera about their difficulty in keeping female athletes who don't make the travel squad, even when they are receiving some financial aid. Coaches have also talked about their difficulty in filling the minimum number of positions desired by the athletic director to achieve proportionality, often because the minimum demands more players than the sport itself requires.

Men's teams, on the other hand, are often no longer allowed to keep any of the numerous men seeking walk-on positions. Further, many schools have capped the number of men on team rosters, usually at numbers far lower than a competitive program needs. For example, before the team was cut in 2007, the men's track and cross-country team at James Madison University was capped at 80 runners, while the women's team was allowed 130 slots. Coach Dave Rinker told *Inside Higher Ed* that he regularly had to turn away "pretty good guys who just want to walk-on and have the experience of college athletics." The marginal cost of such players is small, so schools do not save a significant amount of money by capping rosters. The schools are simply afraid that such spots will skew the overall gender balance, putting the institutions at an increased risk of a Title IX compliance review or private lawsuit.

Physiological differences also contribute to men's and women's level of interest in organized sports. There is substantial research on testosterone to indicate that its presence will impact interest in sports as a participant, as well as a fan. It stands to reason that if nature takes its course, there will always be more men than women pursuing varsity athletics. . . .

Men's Losses in Collegiate Athletics

Proponents of Title IX constantly say that schools can comply with the law by increasing opportunities for women, without cutting opportunities for men. The data, however, point to significant across-the-board damage to men's athletics since Title IX's inception.

In spring 2007, the College Sports Council (CSC) launched a longitudinal study looking at 2.5 years of athletic participation data to determine program trends. The study confirmed that opportunities for men have faced consistent and significant decline under Title IX.

Past studies of athletic participation numbers show an increase in opportunities for both men and women, even while the percentage of schools sponsoring certain sports was decreasing. The flaw in such studies is that they failed to account for the number of NCAA [National Collegiate Athletic Association] schools. Each year, the NCAA admits more schools as NCAA members, which inflates the program numbers. These are not new teams but rather existing teams that are now figured into the NCAA's calculations. The College Sports Council study controlled for that variable using a fixed-year analysis (which is similar to how economists account for inflation).

Once the CSC controlled for that factor, the trend became clear: Across the board, opportunities for women were increasing, while opportunities for men were decreasing. From 1981 to 2005, male athletes per school declined 6%, and men's teams per school dropped 17%. Meanwhile, female athletes per school rose 34%, and women's teams per school rose 34%. The total number of women's teams has exceeded the number of men's teams since 1995.

Every male sport, with the exception of baseball, has decreased or remained static. Non-revenue sports such as wrestling, tennis, and gymnastics have been the hardest hit. . . . Men's gymnastics is practically extinct, with fewer than 20 varsity programs left in the country. . . .

The Football Issue

Proponents of the Title IX status quo would like us to believe that the reason so many schools are dropping non-revenue men's sports is because the schools want to keep their football teams and that football eats up too many resources. Additionally, feminists posit the false statistic that fewer than 20% of football teams are profitable and suggest a radical overhaul of football to be less competitive and more feminine, i.e., less focused on winning and more focused on collaborative play.

The truth is, when the resources are invested to create a competitive program, football helps women. A *Social Science Quarterly* article by Patrick James Rishe concluded that women's sports at schools with big football programs fared better than women's sports at schools with smaller football programs. While Rishe's research does verify what the quota proponents tell us—expenditures are higher for football players than for any other sport—the research also calculates that where the football expenditures are highest, so, too, are the expenditures on female athletes.

In another study by Donald E. Agthe and R. Bruce Billings for the *Journal of Sport Management*, the authors concluded that football profits were a significant influence on achieving financial gender equity in athletic departments.

The *Chronicle of Higher Education* found a similar pattern when it examined Division I schools with and without football programs:

> While women's sports are clearly on the rise across the board, the rate of growth varies widely among the different kinds of colleges in Division I. Wealthy sports programs can subsidize new opportunities and greater spending for women, but those without revenue-producing football and basketball teams lag. And the gap between the haves and the have-nots is widening.

Some have suggested that schools should curtail football and scale the number of positions down to 65, or even down to the 45 carried by professional teams. This suggestion reveals an appalling lack of understanding of the game of football. The collegiate ceiling of 85 football scholarships is already too tight. It has forced coaches to play freshmen who are unaccustomed to the caliber of physical play and the psychological balance of becoming a college student and athlete. It affects the ability of coaches to run a full practice schedule, especially in the spring when the outgoing players are gone, and the incoming players are still in high school. The pros, on the other hand, command an unlimited supply of mature players. When an NFL [National Football League] player is injured or waived, management picks up the phone and brings in a replacement.

Football is not the issue causing schools to drop men's sports. The Title IX gender quota drives schools to drop men's programs despite the schools' best efforts and fervent wishes for keeping all teams intact. Even when there is no football team to blame, men still suffer. That is not equal opportunity.

The College Sports Council study shows that even football has seen a decline in the Title IX era. . . . The percentage of NCAA member schools with football teams has declined since 1980.

How the Status Quo Shortchanges Women

This misapplication of Title IX undermines women as well as men.

When the *Kelley* [*Kelley v. Board of Trustees of the University of Illinois*, 1994] court ruled that there was nothing in Title IX requiring schools to expand or add programs for women in order to comply with the gender quota, the court effectively allowed for the stagnation of women's sports. For example, a school with nine women's teams and 12 men's teams can meet the gender quota simply by cutting enough men to match the number of women on existing teams. There is no need to add any more women's teams, regardless of interest, ability, or market forces.

The OCR [Office of Civil Rights] also encouraged the stagnation of women's sports in the 1996 clarification of the three-prong test. In that document, the OCR defined prong two—history and expansion of women's sports—as only counting the addition of new women's teams. So, if a school has 10 women's teams that are all underfunded, it gains no credit with the government under prong two for expanding the funding or facilities of the 10 existing women's teams. The choice again seems to be eliminate enough men to reach the gender quota or add another women's team that will be underfunded as well.

By allowing, and even encouraging, schools to set high minimums for women's teams, coaches are finding themselves taking on some substandard players to beef up the roster. This affects the competitiveness of women's teams, as well as their morale. It cannot be good for women's sports markets in the long term to field noncompetitive teams. This phenomenon is especially prevalent in sports such as crew, where the participants may have no varsity team experience and require more of the coach's attention just to learn basic skills.

The current application of Title IX also discourages the growth of women's sports in the overall marketplace. The adage that "if you build it, they will come" has not proved true. However, the OCR policies do not provide the flexibility for schools to truly be a part of building new markets for women's sports, including the establishment of club teams to build both interest and ability. Building a market for any sport takes time and some measure of creativity. The focus on participation quotas ignores the need to allow a market to grow. Today's collegiate and high school sports teams compete with the entire entertainment industry to attract players and fans.

By advocating a gender quota, feminists may be undermining true athletic progress for women. Allowing schools to find creative ways to build strong programs and strong marketplaces for women's sports would be better for all women.

Periodical Bibliography

The following articles have been selected to supplement the diverse views presented in this chapter.

Joe Barrett   "University Loses Sioux Mascot War," *Wall Street Journal*, April 10, 2010.

Lucy M. Caldwell   "Are Jocks Necessary?" *Harvard Crimson*, March 7, 2008.

J.P. Giglio and Robbi Pickeral   "Researchers Say NCAA Needs Head-Injury Rules," *News & Observer* (Raleigh, NC), December 5, 2009.

Rene A. Henry   "Will Greed Kill College Sports?" Huntington News Network (West Virginia), June 21, 2010. www.huntingtonnews.net.

Jay Johnson and Margery Holman   "Gender and Hazing: The Same but Different," *JOPERD—The Journal of Physical Education, Recreation & Dance*, May 2009.

Elinor Nauen   "A Sporting Chance: Title IX and the Seismic Shift in Women's Sports," *America*, October 20, 2008.

Bill Penington   "Fair Play? James Madison University's Decision to Eliminate 10 Sports Teams—Mostly Men's—to Comply with a Federal 'Gender Equity' Law Is the Latest Chapter in the Debate over the Fairness of Title IX," *New York Times Upfront*, January 15, 2007.

Mark Rinaldi   "Ouch! Study Says Some Sports Injuries Are No Accident," HarrisonPatch, June 18, 2010. http://harrison.patch.com.

Dave Solomon   "Quinnipiac Title IX Trial Begins on Monday," *New Haven Register* (Connecticut), June 20, 2010.

Jill Lieber Steeg et al.   "College Athletes' Studies Guided Toward 'Major in Eligibility,'" *USA Today*, November 19, 2008.

OPPOSING
VIEWPOINTS®
SERIES

CHAPTER 4

What Issues Do Greek Letter Organizations Face?

Chapter Preface

Rachel Pappas, class of 2007, was happy to be a sister in the Delta Zeta sorority chapter at DePauw University, until she received a letter from the national office informing her that she had been put on alumna status (retired from active membership) and would have to move out of the sorority house in the middle of the school year; she was one of twenty-three Delta Zetas in a chapter of thirty-five to be evicted. The letter explained that she hadn't helped enough with new member recruitment, although the only women in the group penalized for lack of effort happened to also be the members who were overweight or not Caucasian. Six more students resigned in protest before the university closed the sorority's doors on campus; DePauw president Robert G. Bottoms reprimanded Delta Zeta for its poor timing and insensitivity to the sorority members' academic needs.

Greek letter organizations, particularly traditional fraternities and sororities, have long struggled against stereotypes that portray their members as shallow, vapid partners interested only in drinking and sex; members proudly point instead to their legacies of community service, commitments to academic achievement, and the lifelong friendships and support networks that develop among their houses. In fact, the Delta Zeta national organization establishes on its Web site that the purpose of the sorority is to "unite its members in the bonds of sincere and lasting friendship, to stimulate one another in the pursuit of knowledge, to promote the moral and social culture of its members, and to develop plans for guidance and unity in action." The Web page devoted to the sorority's "visual standards" refer only to how the sorority logo and letterhead should be printed on stationery and envelopes. Rachel Pappas told *Cosmopolitan* magazine in June 2007, however, that the members of Delta Zeta at DePauw—the "Dog House" by reputation—had been visited by representatives from the national organization who ran two-day fashion workshops and gave makeup lessons. They were told that there was no reason to ever appear on campus without wearing at least mascara and lip gloss.

Representatives of the national Delta Zeta organization denied that the women asked to leave the sorority at DePauw University were put on alumna status because of their looks. On March 28, 2007, executive director Cindy Menges told *USA Today* that low enrollment was the primary concern over the DePauw chapter; the terms of the sorority's charter required ninety-five members, but at DePauw membership had fallen to thirty-five. Menges emphasized that the members of the DePauw chapter were not interested in working hard to recruit new members, and they cared more about their individual experiences as Delta Zetas than their contributions to the national group. Delta Zeta gave the members at DePauw a space to form friendships and nurture their personal interests, but the members at DePauw did not appreciate the effort required to maintain the sorority house in the first place.

Alexandra Robbins, in her March 5, 2007, article for the *New Republic*, suggests that Delta Zeta's actions could be seen as a prudent business decision (if also a cruel public relations disaster). She cites research that suggests women who base their self-esteem on appearance are more likely to join sororities in the first place, and she explains that such potential members are going to look for groups that reflect an image they would like to maintain. Delta Zeta needed to attract new members to pay their house's expenses; a prettier chapter would have appealed to many more candidates in the recruitment pool. It's a pragmatic approach to a financial problem, Robbins suggests, though it is at odds with its stated goals of enriching women's moral culture and supporting sincere friendships. Robbins points out that "sororities often forget that they are members of a university community" and too often treat members like "disposable income" rather than sisters.

The following chapter examines other campus issues that affect how Greek letter organizations are perceived by society at large, how fraternities and sororities respond to those perceptions, and how leaders and members balance decades of tradition with finding solutions to modern problems.

"Joining the Greek system gives you a chance to join up and associate with like-minded individuals, which enriches your total college experience."

Membership in a Greek Letter Organization Enhances the College Experience

Sarah Gwin

Sarah Gwin graduated from Florida State University in 2009, where she was a staff writer for the FSView & Florida Flambeau, *an independent campus newspaper that is distributed all over the city of Tallahassee. The following viewpoint ran in the first issue of the school year, during the recruitment period for new fraternity and sorority members. Gwin interviews men and women who have already joined Greek organizations about their experiences, and she presents a positive picture of the potential benefits of membership, from taking on leadership roles to giving back to the community to always having a set of close friends.*

Sarah Gwin, "Is Going Greek Worth It?" *FSView & Florida Flambeau*, vol. 15, August 21, 2006, p.24. Copyright © 2006 by FSView & Florida Flambeau. All rights reserved. Reproduced by permission.

As you read, consider the following questions:

1. How much money and time does Gwin say fraternities and sororities at Florida State University donated to charities during a recent year?

2. What is the Order of Omega, and what does it demonstrate, according to Gwin?

3. According to Gwin, what percentage of the students at Florida State University are members of a fraternity or sorority?

With so many students attending Florida State [University, FSU], it is hard to find somewhere to fit in. Many students pick the path of going Greek to find their place. There are 20 Interfraternity Council [IFC] men fraternities and 15 Panhellenic Association women sororities that are recognized by FSU. There are also nine National Pan-Hellenic Council fraternities and sororities which are predominantly African American and seven Multicultural Greek Council fraternities and sororities.

Fall is a busy time for sororities and fraternities to gain new members. Panhellenic recruitment started Aug. 20 [2006], and IFC rush begins Sept. 11. Pledging is a huge choice for college students to make. It does have some financial obligations and there are many meetings and events to attend. Is going Greek worth all that time and money? Many students think that it is.

"Being a Greek is not cheap and it does take up a lot of my time," FSU senior Sjanna Henderson said. "I have to have a job to help pay for my sorority. But, without Kappa I would not have survived college. I found a place where I belong in FSU, a home with my sisters."

Opportunities for Growth

Joining a frat or a sorority provides college students with many benefits such as leadership opportunities. There

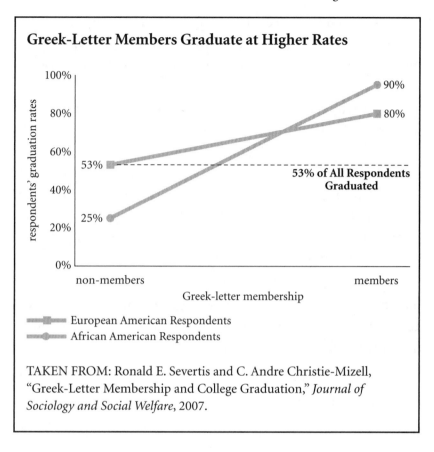

Greek-Letter Members Graduate at Higher Rates

respondents' graduation rates (y-axis): 0%, 20%, 40%, 60%, 80%, 100%

53%

25%

90%

80%

53% of All Respondents
Graduated

Greek-letter membership (x-axis): non-members — members

European American Respondents
African American Respondents

TAKEN FROM: Ronald E. Severtis and C. Andre Christie-Mizell, "Greek-Letter Membership and College Graduation," *Journal of Sociology and Social Welfare*, 2007.

are over 400 leadership positions in the Greek community alone.

"As a result of participating in recruitment I made a family of friends. Being Greek was one of my best decisions; it has allowed me to grow as a person and as a leader," external VP of the Greek Activities Council and FSU senior Lindsay Opsah said. "When I went through recruitment, I was looking for a place to lead and be led—I definitely found that in my sisters. I feel that ADPi [Alpha Delta Pi] has been a major factor in my growth into adulthood. Even if you don't pledge, recruitment is a way to meet people and see what being Greek is all about."

It is difficult to meet new people by just going to class or randomly saying hello to a nice-looking person. Going through rush and recruitment helps students to make friends more easily.

"I actually went through rush to meet new people and it was probably the best decision of my life," FSU junior Nikki Stewart said. "Being in Zeta has allowed me to meet an amazing group of girls and give back to my community through our philanthropy. The statement I came to college to find my bridesmaid is so true because these girls will forever be a part of my life. They have allowed me to find my niche at FSU and have accepted me for who I am."

In addition, sororities and fraternities take pride in how they help others. The entire Greek community at FSU raised and donated over $100,000 and 30,000 service hours to charities over the past academic year.

A Rich Social Life

Being in a frat or a sorority also leaves little time for boredom. There are many activities for Greeks and they are encouraged to join other clubs.

"What I like about being in a frat is that you always have something to do, whether it's socials, formals, meetings, intramural sports, philanthropies, etc.," FSU senior and Fiji member John Kruszewski said. "Once you are in Greek life it is also a lot easier to get involved around campus."

Academic success is also very important to Greeks. Each organization requires a minimum grade point average to remain an active member of the chapter. The Greek community even created the Order of Omega, its own honorary group, to recognize the scholastic achievements of Greek men and women.

Building a Larger Greek Community

However, even with all the good things about Greek life, no organization is without problems. The Greek community is still struggling to be the best it can be.

"As nervous and ignorant as I was when rushing I have always had good feelings and high expectations for the Greek community here at Florida State," FSU president of Phi Kappa Psi and junior Leeroy Habern said. "We have so much potential to be one of the greatest in the nation. However, it seems as if we're constantly fighting each other; which has been holding everyone back. While the Greek life at other campuses are struggling to become more unified and stronger, I feel as if Florida State is running in circles with our own individual struggles to create a distinctive separation from each fraternity/sorority. I truly feel that all of our chapters here are full of some of the finest men and women in the nation and I am proud to be a part of that. However, no progress will ever be made until we realize that having a few good chapters is nothing compared to having an amazing Greek community."

Benefits Outweigh Drawbacks

However, with all the benefits the Greek life provides, it is not for everyone. Many students are not willing to spend money and their time to be Greek.

"I guess the reason I didn't rush, is that anytime I thought of a fraternity, it made me think of things I would be giving up, and simple economics tells me to take the better deal; when I could be at the smelly, dirty, sticky, frat house, I'd rather be at home, spending time with my girl," FSU senior Houston Spear said. "Don't get me wrong, I love Greek life, and I think that everyone should try it at least once, who knows, you might just fall in love with the experience."

Going Greek has its downfalls but it also has many advantages. It is a big decision and commitment for a student to decide to pledge. The 14 percent of the full-time undergraduate population of FSU students that have chosen the Greek way of life believe that the choice they made is worth it.

"Going Greek is the best decision I've made aside from becoming a Seminole," FSU junior and Sigma Chi member Alexander Monroe Regar said. "I went through rush because I was tired of passing around the hat for money for parties, and I was tired of going to random house parties and hanging out with people I didn't really have anything in common with. Joining the Greek system gives you a chance to join up and associate with like-minded individuals, which enriches your total college experience."

> *"Factors in their decisions to quit were organizational difficulties, interpersonal relationships . . . , membership/role-taking expectations, time requirements and financial obligations."*

Sororities Are Out of Touch with Today's Members

Elizabeth Leigh Farrington

Elizabeth Leigh Farrington is the associate publisher of Women in Higher Education, *a monthly news journal about the role of women in academia. In the following viewpoint, she summarizes research presented at a Student Affairs Administrators conference about declining sorority membership. Although students affiliated with Greek organizations are more likely to stay in college, they report dropping out of their groups because they do not feel supported academically and because they find many of the mandatory scheduled activities a poor use of their time. Farrington provides suggestions for how to increase membership by modernizing sororities' structures to make them more relevant to today's college students.*

Elizabeth Leigh Farrington, "How to Help Sororities Survive in Today's World," *Women in Higher Education*, vol. 18, July 2009, p. 22–23. Copyright © 2009 Women in Higher Education. Reproduced by permission.

As you read, consider the following questions:

1. When did Renee Wiedenhoeft first become interested in the sorority attrition rate, according to Farrington?

2. According to the author, how has the failure to evolve put modern sororities so out of touch with women's values?

3. What recommendation does Wiedenhoeft have for updating how sororities function?

Although much has been written about the negative impact of Greek life on campus, membership in a sorority can offer many benefits for women, including a sense of community, support and engagement. This can also pay off in increased student retention rates.

Yet many sororities cling to outdated models that don't recognize the changing nature of today's students, resulting in increased attrition. Why are women leaving sororities, and what can campuses do to help them to create environments in which college women can flourish?

Renee Wiedenhoeft, a residence hall director at Marquette University [Wisconsin], and Becky Druetzler, director of Greek life at Butler University [Indiana], each presented her research on sorority attrition in "So Long, Sister: Examining Panhellenic Sorority Membership Attrition" at a session at the NASPA [National Association of Student Personnel Administrators] conference in Seattle in March [2009].

Wiedenhoeft's doctoral dissertation at Bowling Green [State University, BGSU] resulted from her membership in the Delta Zeta sorority there, where one-third of members quit in one year. She wanted to know why. Her research questions were: What motivated women to join sororities? What were their perceptions of the benefits of membership? Was it all about partying? And what were the factors related to membership withdrawal?

Druetzler's study resulted from her VP wanting data on what was going on with sororities and fraternities. Looking at nine years of retention data, she found students affiliated with Greek groups had a 10–15% higher retention rate from freshman to senior year than those who weren't affiliated.

Research has shown that female peer groups are key to college student organizations. Greek members are more engaged with their schools, which leads to increased donor dollars down the road. "It's easy to focus on the negative, such as binge drinking, but institutions need to be cognitive of the positive effects of membership," they said.

Sisters at Bowling Green State University

Wiedenhoeft's study at Bowling Green was drawn from a pool of 265 women who were initiated into a sorority in fall 2006. One year later, 88 members had quit and only 177 remained active members, a loss of one-third of new members over one year. Some quit after only one week.

Offering them $25 gift cards to participate, she met with eight current, active sorority women, whom she interviewed for an hour as a focus group. From them she got contact info for 25 women who had left a sorority after joining in fall 2006. Six of the women agreed to participate, and she interviewed them individually for 45 minutes each. "It was a snowball sample," she said.

It's tempting to attribute attrition to financial reasons. But her advisor asked, if they say financial reasons led them to leave, is it true or is it a safe, fallback excuse?

Working with three other graduate students and her advisor, she identified key themes from the focus groups:

Active members. They reported attachment and engagement, were connected to the organization and the other women, and felt valued. They formed relationships; their sorority sisters were their best friends. These women also joined for self-knowledge and leadership experience, either as a chair or chapter president or as an alumnae advisor.

Former members. These women experienced conflict and disconnection, feeling unconnected right after joining, and that the sorority was not a good fit. "I was looking for a group that I'd be best friends with, but they wanted me to be too close to them," said one woman. "I was expected to do too much."

Factors in their decisions to quit were organizational difficulties, interpersonal relationships (conflicts with other members, including fights over boyfriends), membership/role-taking expectations, time requirements and financial obligations. Finances were a much greater factor than just handing over a check. For many, the cost-benefit analysis didn't measure up.

When joining any organization, members take on a role and try to figure out how to act, she said. Women bristled at being told that formal recruitment (also known as "rush," which can last three weeks or more) was expected to take precedence over academics. Time requirements forced the women to choose between the sorority and academics, the newspaper, athletics and internships.

Sisters at Butler University

Butler University has had Greeks on campus for more than 150 years—since 1874. Today about 35% of its almost 4,000 students are Greeks, including 40% of the first-year students. All seven sororities on campus have houses. Most are service-oriented: Together Greek students logged 28,000 service hours and raised $100,000 for local groups. For fall semester 2008, campus Greeks averaged a 3.45 GPA [grade point average].

With so large a Greek presence on Butler's campus, Druetzler's concerns about perceptions of trust led her to design an anonymous, online survey rather than a face-to-face format. She sent an online survey to 56 students who had left their sororities, and received 25 back. She found:

- 92% of respondents joined as first-year students

- 80% joined their first choice chapter

- 56% mentioned the members as their reason to join

- 68% had lived in the chapter house

- 36% left as juniors (the largest group)

- 20% had held a leadership position in the chapter

Why did they want to join a sorority?

- 88% wanted friendship and social opportunities

- 76% sought involvement

- 52% cited values of the national group

- 72% said service opportunities

- 68% sought leadership opportunities

- 64% sought networking

- 28% cited academic support

How well were their needs met? On a scale of one to five, most rated these factors in the range of three; "academic support" got the most votes for needs "not met at all."

The largest group of women (28%) reported starting to feel disconnected at the end of their first semester of sophomore year. The women had to live in the dorms their first year, and recruitment at Butler is in January, so this reflects the end of three semesters in the sorority, and the end of the first semester of living in the sorority house. What influenced the women to quit?

- Time commitment 76%

- Expectations of members 64%

- Requirements to live in the sorority house 60%

- Financial reasons 44%

Ex-members also cited conflicts between personal values and values of other members (20%), time commitments (20%), and financial reasons (24%) as the most important factors influencing their decisions.

Personal statements were also telling. At BGSU, women said, "Members stopped being nice to us once we initiated." It was a shock because it was incongruent with the sorority's supposed values: The women thought that after joining members would be nicer and more welcoming to them. One woman said she didn't want to put her time into something she didn't really enjoy.

At Butler, women said the sorority did not value their academic goals. A commuter student said the sorority was way too great of a time commitment. One said the experience was exactly what she'd hoped to avoid in college. Another said she didn't fit in with her pledge class—even though she tried "really hard." Another cited a huge requirement to find time to do sorority activities.

A domino effect hit at Butler—when one woman left, others followed. When others left the house to study abroad, others were brought in to fill that spot.

One former member said she wished someone had explained during recruitment that she'd have to live in the sorority house for two years; national guidelines required only one year. During rush, she wasn't allowed to talk to potential members; instead, they made her check coats so she couldn't have any real contact with potential members. . . .

One Sorority Sister Pulls Rank, One Sorority Sister Quits

For Beth, a conflict with a social event resulted in a breaking point for her membership satisfaction. A date party [was] held at a local bar where those who were underage could not attend, so the attendance turned out to be very low. The member who planned the event vocalized her frustration via an e-mail to the entire chapter. Beth thought it would be appropriate to send an e-mail explaining why many women, including herself, did not attend the event, but she was met with an unexpected response:

... [The social chair] said, "well if you have a problem then you set up a meeting with me." ... The meeting turned into not me expressing my opinions but her telling me that I'm a brand-new pledge so I don't know anything about the sorority, so basically my opinions were moot. She just really attacked me.... "You don't know anything; your concerns are invalid." That just really made me sit back and wonder, Is this what it's going to be like? ... She didn't take any of my concerns and didn't make any plans for suggestions I had.

Renee M. Piquette-Wiedenhoeft, "A Qualitative Study of Panhellenic Sorority Membership Attrition," August 2008.

Female Relationships

Wiedenhoeft concluded that sororities are women's groups modeled after men's. But women have different values: They seek to maintain relationships instead of seeking justice.

She found evidence of self-silencing to pursue that goal. Women told her, "I just can't fight it anymore."

The whole idea of mandatory requirements made the women really angry. There were checklists of obligations, such as a specific number of community service hours required—with fines and other punishments for missing events or failing to meet obligations. Why are so many things mandatory, asked Wiedenhoeft?

The problem is that sororities haven't evolved from their creation more than 150 years ago. College women have changed their values and priorities. Access to college and the reasons women are attracted to higher education have changed. Today's college women also arrive with increased research and knowledge, and they have other training and development opportunities besides sororities. Yet chapters continue to operate under outdated models.

Formal recruitment procedures also haven't adapted to the times. Potential members meet only five or six of the sorority's 50 members, an inadequate cross section. The selection and pledging process is also outmoded because the old model of a member being "chosen" no longer applies, she said. Today, members are consumers. If they aren't happy, they'll leave. Sororities are no longer the only link to campus life—they're now just one slice of the pie.

The women need a highly relational experience. The higher education and fraternal communities need to understand the membership needs of women's peer groups, and to adopt practices to support those needs, using theories about women, student development and the organization.

It's crucial that sororities make sure the membership experience is consistent with their perceptions of the benefits of membership and motivations for joining, through continual evaluation and membership development. This includes educating potential members about the real experiences and obligations they'll have.

Revamp or Retire

Wiedenhoeft recommends that sororities and potential members make their selections according to values, not social status, and that sororities shift their emphasis from checklists of obligations to creating relationships. One session participant knew of a sorority that divided its members into three groups, and spread the requirements among them, so each member had fewer responsibilities.

Based on her research, Druetzler recommends that campuses intervene to support sororities in retaining their members. It starts with educating potential members on what to expect, and how to find a chapter that fits their needs. "We do exit interviews with students in general," she said, "but that's too late. By then the marriage is over. We need ongoing conversations, and more frequent."

Sharing these assessments with the sorority's members is crucial, said Wiedenhoeft. Often during interviews with active members, they asked her, "Why are they leaving?"

Conflict resolution training may be another solution, said Druetzler. For new members who discover that they don't support the sorority's activities, teaching them how to navigate the waters may prove beneficial. Don't count on sorority advisers, she warned. They have real jobs and with 100 members to keep track of, they can get jaded.

The solution to creating sorority houses that support and nurture women may be found on your own campus. If you can connect with a sorority that's been successful at retaining members, find out what they're doing right, and what you can learn from them. One place to start may be with historically black sororities, which tend to focus more on values, leadership development and academic support.

> *"Greeks on college campuses are in some instances twice as likely to drink while underage and use illegal drugs as non-Greek students."*

Greek Members Are More Likely to Binge Drink and Use Drugs

Ashlei N. Stevens

Ashlei N. Stevens is a writer for the Spartanburg Herald-Journal; *she has also written for the* New York Times. *In the following viewpoint, she reports on the findings of a study of substance abuse in South Carolina. Study commissioners noted that members of Greek organizations—college fraternities and sororities—reported binge drinking, drinking and driving, and using drugs at much higher rates than the student population as a whole. Stevens explores how such alcohol and drug use behavior would be considered problematic outside of the university setting, and she shares some ways that schools are attempting to curb drinking on campus.*

As you read, consider the following questions:

1. What is the difference between the percentage of Greek students who binge drink and the percentage of all students and athletes who binge drink, according to the study Stevens cites?

2. According to Erin Morgan at the University of South Carolina Upstate, how are heavy-drinking behaviors perceived differently at college than they are everywhere else?

3. What are some steps Stevens describes that have been taken at Wofford College to curb reckless drinking among Greek organization members?

College fraternity and sorority members are sometimes stereotyped as lively students known for their keg parties, and a new study suggests that this may be partly true. Greeks on college campuses are in some instances twice as likely to drink while underage and use illegal drugs as non-Greek students.

That's according to a report conducted by the State Epidemiological Outreach Workgroup (SEOW), which was released recently by Spartanburg Alcohol and Drug Abuse Commission [SADAC]. SEOW examined information on alcohol, drug, tobacco and other data to examine substance abuse in South Carolina. Each of the 46 counties received an individual report, which includes data on teen pregnancy, crime, truancy, and substance abuse.

Out of the nearly 50-page report, SADAC officials said they were most surprised by the high rates at which fraternity and sorority members binge drink, drink while driving, and use illegal drugs. A survey was given to 390 students at an anonymous college in Spartanburg County. Of those 390 students, 273 were ages 17 to 20.

Drinking and Drug Use on Campus

In 2007, the study shows that 65 percent of all students and athletes used alcohol within the past 30 days, while that number is close to 90 percent for Greeks. Half of freshmen surveyed had used alcohol within the past month.

Binge drinking rates were also noticeably higher with Greeks. Binge alcohol use is defined as five or more drinks on a single occasion. While just above 40 percent of all students and athletes admitted to binge drinking within the past two weeks of the survey, close to 80 percent of Greeks admitted to binge drinking.

"It's alarming to us because of the fact that they're underage," said SADAC prevention specialist Gregg McCullough, "and also with the illegal substances like cocaine and marijuana, it's just a high percentage—much higher than what you'd find in the general population."

In 2007, the study found that 45 percent of Greeks used marijuana in the past year, compared with 25 percent of all other students, about 24 percent of freshmen, and 15 percent of athletes. Roughly twenty percent of Greeks used some drug other than marijuana in the past year, compared with about eight percent of all other students.

Numbers were high for Greeks who drink and drive. Fifty-four percent of Greeks admitted to drinking and driving, compared with 34 percent of all other students. And more Greeks have been arrested for driving under the influence—13 percent—compared with just 4 percent of student athletes and 2 percent of freshmen, the study found.

"The biggest concern is that in college—at age 18, 19, 20—your brain is still developing and doesn't finish maturing until the early 20s or mid 20s," McCullough said. "And to introduce these substances is throwing a big wrench in their development. The earlier you use these substances, the more likely you'll have dependency problems on these drugs."

McCullough said SADAC plans to establish a collaborative panel of officials from each of the county's colleges to find ways to prevent underage drinking and substance abuse. Student life coordinators at a few local colleges admit that a problem exists. They said this study closely mirrors national data, which often suggests that Greek students use drugs and alcohol more frequently than other college students.

"It's definitely a problem," said Erin Morgan, who coordinates the drug and alcohol program at the University of South Carolina Upstate [USC], adding that freshmen and student-athletes are also in the high-risk group.

Morgan noted that many students' perception is that "drinking is just seen as a rite of passage—it's kind of like 'everybody does it in college—that's what you do,'" she said. "If you take it out of the college setting, and were in the real world, they would have a full-blown addiction or alcohol problem. They don't realize that once they graduate, it doesn't stop."

Morgan is a certified counselor who presents workshops and activities on drug and alcohol awareness. An interest meeting was held on campus last fall to discuss creating an anonymous alcohol and drug recovery group, because the need is there, she said.

Starting Younger

"What some of the national data is showing is that students are actually coming to college with addiction problems already established," Morgan said. "Kids are starting to use and get addicted younger and younger."

Fortunately, there have never been any drug- or alcohol-related deaths at USC Upstate, nor at Wofford College, officials said. In December, an 18-year-old Clemson University student died after binge drinking at an off-campus fraternity house, and authorities said he had at least four times the legal limit of alcohol to drive in his system. That incident has

Fraternity and Sorority Binge Drinking at the University of Iowa

"Greek" first-year students were 1.8 times more likely to binge drink at least once in a typical two-week period than nonaffiliated students. For seniors who were members of fraternities and sororities, the odds of binge drinking at least once in a typical two-week period were 2.4 times that of their nonaffiliated peers. . . .

The significant positive relationship between Greek affiliation and binge drinking frequency was the same for students who reported they did not binge drink in high school as for students who reported they did. We infer from this that the significant influence of fraternity/sorority affiliation on binge drinking is an effect of socialization, rather than of recruitment. Even when levels of reported high school binge drinking (as well as other potential influences) were taken into account, Greek affiliation increased substantially the odds that a student would binge drink in college. Though fraternities and sororities at the University of Iowa might not recruit binge drinkers, they appear to create them.

Elizabeth Whitt et al.,
"Research on Iowa Student Experiences:
Binge Drinking," RISE Brief no. 2, October 2008.

prompted discussions about stepping up awareness, said Roberta Bigger, vice president for students at Wofford.

"We can't do enough education with the students," Bigger said.

Wofford serves 1,350 students and almost half of them are in Greek life. Underage drinking does happen, but, because the fraternity houses are located on campus, as are many of the social events, drinking and driving isn't a big issue, officials said.

Courtney Shelton is Wofford's director of student activities and Greek life. Officers within each of the 13 Greek letter organizations go through training at the beginning of each semester. To ensure accountability, the college has "sober party officers," who monitor parties and turn in names to Shelton's office of those engaging in underage drinking.

"We want them to be able to be educated and know what their liability is and their responsibility for their fellow student," Shelton said.

The college has counseling and referral services, too.

"I think it's an issue. I don't want to paint an issue that our students are absolutely perfect," Bigger said. "We have our challenges."

In fact, a student can confidentially refer a friend to counseling or health services. And the bond that fraternity and sorority members share within their group often prompts one member to encourage another to get help with a problem, Shelton said.

"That's definitely one of the strengths of any Greek organization: They do have close relationships and accountability," Shelton said. "They're aware when something's not going right with one of their friends or chapter members, so they're very comfortable going to health services to refer a friend."

> *"I don't know that anybody would run and pay . . . to see a movie about a sorority experience that talks about the leadership aspect, the academic aspect, the community service aspect."*

Greek Letter Organizations Are Unfairly Portrayed in Popular Culture

Sarah Ball

Sarah Ball is an arts and entertainment reporter for Newsweek .com and Newsweek *magazine. She primarily covers film and pop culture, but she has also written about politics, health, and the fine arts. The following viewpoint appeared in response to the publicity for the movie* Sorority Row, *the latest installment of a series of films that portrays sorority members as vapid, hypersexual creatures with frivolous interests. Ball makes the point that actual sorority life would make boring entertainment, and she lauds the television show* Greek *for presenting Greek organizations as clubs full of students with complicated personalities and diverse ambitions.*

As you read, consider the following questions:

1. According to Ball, what is the typical film and television portrayal of a sorority member?

2. According to Lawrence Ross, why are sororities easy targets for stereotypes and criticism?

3. What does the creator of the television show *Greek* say about his approach to Greek stereotypes?

You won't recognize most of the cleavage-baring cast of *Sorority Row*. Maybe you've seen Rumer Willis, the famous daughter of Bruce Willis and Demi Moore. Or Audrina Patridge, that girl from *The Hills*. The others? Solidly unknown.

But you're probably familiar with the most important supporting cast member: squishy, gel-filled bra inserts.

"I'm only A, so I'm, like, super-tiny, so you put some A-[cup] chicken cutlets in and a padded B bra, and you're set. You've got, like, Ds," says actress Briana Evigan of her boob-boosting costume requirements for the role, in a videotaped junket for the horror film. Willis, meanwhile, talks at length about her fear of the padded inserts falling out.

Even the male director, Stewart Hendler, weighs in. "[The studio] wanted as much skin as possible, 'cause it's an R-rated movie, and you want to deliver to the audience that signs up for that," Hendler says in the junket video. "I definitely didn't want to make a movie that was exploitative and misogynistic . . . but I definitely had pressure, like, 'Why don't you have a girl just pull off her top?'" (Hendler did not respond to *Newsweek*'s request for comment through the movie's studio, Summit Entertainment).

You're probably not surprised—and why would you be? If there is a shop-worn template for any character in movies and television, it's the sorority girl. She's blonde, busty, and artificially tan. Her daywear involves a lot of mix-and-match pink—plus Greek letters, of course. Her major is incidental, but her weekend plans are not: there's the mall, then the bars, then the bedroom of some fraternity guy who doesn't know her last name.

Who could defend her?

Realism Doesn't Sell Movie Tickets

Well, me. I was in a sorority. I don't know anyone who fits the cliché described above, and I know a lot of sorority girls: my sister, mother, aunts, grandmother and grand-aunts were all in them. Most of my female relatives attended college before campuses were co-ed, and sororities were one of few extracurricular options for women. "There was cheerleading, and a few girls on the tennis or swimming team, but not much else," my mom recalls of her years in school. To her and the rest of my family, going Greek wasn't a willing submission to objectification and tanning beds—it was more like attending all-girls summer camp, minus the mosquito bites.

Not that a movie about playing kickball and brushing each other's hair would get the studio green light. Better to watch Barbie bend over: In MTV's reality series *Sorority Life*, recruitment of new members is something akin to a low-rent beauty pageant, for which a potential member might hire a "rush consultant" to pre-select outfits. In *The House Bunny*, a flagging sorority saves itself and its social standing by wearing more makeup and fewer clothes, thanks to instructional tips from a former Playboy bunny. In slasher sequel *Scream 2*, CiCi (Sarah Michelle Gellar) is stabbed to death in her pink cardigan, then dumped over the balcony of her Omega Beta Zeta house. Hey, she was an elitist sorority snob. It's not murder—it's poetic justice.

"I don't know that anybody would run and pay $8 to see a movie about a sorority experience that talks about the leadership aspect, the academic aspect, the community service aspect, the friendship aspect, the health aspect," says Julie

Greek Letter Members Understand the Importance of Community and Citizenship

Nathan, a junior [interviewed for this article], noted, "when you come to college you think you know what is . . . going on in the world," but involvement in fraternity and sorority life is "an eye-opening experience," revealing "opportunities you didn't know existed and seeing how these things have an impact and can improve you as a citizen." He offered as an example his involvement in a service project in which his fraternity served dinner to the homeless. This experience challenged him to reflect on his own privilege. . . . He began to consider the "big picture," meaning his awareness of the diversity of lived human experiences within the same city in which he attended college. . . . Brian, a sophomore, shared a similar experience, reflecting upon his alternative spring break trip with his fraternity brothers. He noted that the town where they stayed "was night and day from where we are from. These new experiences help to open your mind to the world."

While service experiences were a prominent example of how one's involvement in a fraternity or sorority impacts an evolving understanding of one's self in a community, other evidence emerged. For example, Derek, a sophomore, described how meetings of the Panhellenic Council and the Interfraternity Congress (the governing boards for the fraternal communities) helped to reveal that each individual is part of something larger. He noted that at these meetings he sees that matters impact more than just him or one chapter. . . .

Amie Jackson and Susan V. Iverson,
"'Step Up and Do It,': Fraternity and Sorority Members'
Beliefs About Citizenship," Oracle: The Research Journal of the
Association of Fraternity Advisors, *February 2009.*

Burkhard, chairman of the National Panhellenic [Conference], a governing organization for 26 member sororities. "Overall, it's a very, very positive experience for young women, but we work every day to try to combat those stereotypes. It's really and truly three steps ahead and two steps back."

It's not just predominantly white groups that are targets. Alpha Kappa Alpha [AKA], the oldest African American sisterhood, was founded as a support group at Howard University for women just one generation out of slavery. But in popular movies like Spike Lee's 1988 *School Daze* or the 2007 dance movie *Stomp the Yard*, fictionalized versions of AKA sisters are seen as little more than midriff-baring arm candy or (in the case of *Daze*) submissive sex minions for fraternity brothers. Lawrence [C.] Ross . . . author of the book *The Divine Nine: The History of African American Fraternities and Sororities*, says any collective of women that sets itself apart risks being conflated with cliques. "[It's] very easy to project anti-women sentiments on [sororities]—it's an easy formula, as much a formula as an African American being the first person killed in a horror film," Ross says. "There's a value added to that either-or choice to join a sorority. There's no value added if you do or don't join student government. . . . But particularly with African American sororities, if you join, then you're judged as being separate from the rest."

A Television Show Avoids Stereotypes

Not every screenwriter takes the cheap shot. Patrick Sean Smith is the creator and executive producer of ABC Family's *Greek*, a sitcom that follows the stories of several characters in fraternities and sororities at an Ohio university. When Smith wrote the pilot, he skipped the misogynistic tropes of *Sorority Row* and went straight for the lightsome tone and bleeding-heart angst of John Hughes movies. "It seemed too easy to go with stereotypes—this felt like a real opportunity to be different," Smith says. "I kind of wanted to start with stereotypes, because I wanted it to be able to translate for people who didn't know the world. I wanted to say, 'Here are these characters you've seen a million times over—but here are the million layers underneath.'"

The result is both effervescent and intelligent, without incurring a toothache—the show's marketing icon is a red, Solo [drinking] cup, synonymous with a good time. The cast is diverse and their narrative threads have depth: a gay brother struggles to come out to his house; a blonde sorority president fights to be taken seriously as a congressional intern. Even without a boost from chicken cutlets, the show is popular. Adult viewership rose 102 percent on last year's [2008's] season 2 premiere, and the network's ad sales rose 96 percent around the same time. (The third season returned Aug. 31 [2009].)

Burkhard says she cautiously approves of the show's take. "I watched it when it first came out, and I can honestly tell you that I do think that there are some positive messages there," she says. "You can tell that their writers have done their research in terms of trying to use terminology correctly, and to portray situations as reality based as they can." Burkhard says that the show's writers haven't contacted the National Panhellenic [Conference] for advice, but "I'd love for them to call me and say, 'Let's talk.'"

As reps from two groups so long at odds, Burkhard and Smith seem to be on the same page: "In this day and age, something that still bases itself in tradition and history is admirable for young people," Smith says. "And for me, I'm never looking to do edge for the sake of edge. I don't want to do exploitative for the sake of exploitative. I like to do real for the sake of real."

For now, he's alright being the rare entertainment executive who gambles that authenticity won't result in tedium. As he puts it, "There's no competition."

"*[Historically Black Greek Letter Organizations] . . . served to provide safe havens in terms of refuge from hostile institutional climates experienced on campus.*"

Membership in Black Greek Organizations Can Be Beneficial

Fred A. Bonner II

Fred A. Bonner II is an associate professor of higher education administration at Texas A&M University, College Station. His publications include articles and book chapters on academically gifted African American male college students, teaching in the multicultural college classroom, and diversity issues in student affairs. In the following viewpoint, Bonner examines Historically Black Greek Letter Organizations (HBGLOs) from a historical perspective. He argues that HBGLOs were envisioned and created in response to racial injustice and provided African American students a safe haven from the racial hostility experienced on campus. These fraternities and sororities continue to function as instruments of social change to this day. Membership in

Fred A. Bonner II, "The Historically Black Greek Letter Organization: Finding a Place and Making a Way," *Black History Bulletin*, vol. 69, no. 1, Winter/Spring 2006, pp. 17–18. Reproduced by permission.

HBGLOs has many benefits for students, including a safe place to foster relationships with peers.

As you read, consider the following questions:

1. When were HBGLOs envisioned and created?
2. How did the social and political environment in the United States contribute to the formation of HBGLOs?
3. Name two examples the author uses to illustrate the benefits of joining HBGLOs.

Apart from churches, fraternal and benevolent societies have long been the largest and most durable organizations in black communities. The founders and leaders of these organizations were in the vanguard of social change and made significant contributions to the widespread liberation, political, moral, temperance, and social reform movements that characterized the nineteenth century United States.

African American history has been greatly influenced by the emergence and development of Historically Black Greek Letter Organizations (HBGLOs). To say that the major advancements in education and civil rights were influenced by these groups is an understatement. A cursory review of the status of Black America will quickly reveal that the past contributions of HBGLOs were significant in elevating the African American condition both domestically and abroad. Consequently, it seems particularly appropriate that the 2006 centennial celebration planned by the first of these organizations, the 100-year-old Alpha Phi Alpha Fraternity, took place in the summer of 2006 in Washington, D.C. In keeping with its central mission, this celebration took place amid a flurry of activities planned by the organization in order to draw attention to the status of African Americans—a topic that HBGLOs have used as their platform since their inception.

A Refuge from a Hostile Climate

To fully appreciate the impact of HBGLOs, it is important to understand the political and societal climate in the United States that prompted their development and their subsequent mission. Specifically, HBGLOs were envisioned and created in the early 1900s during a period in which the national climate upheld racial injustice, inequality, and separate but "*un*-equal" doctrines that marginalized the existence of the African American. During these times, those who dared to forge new boundaries and occupy spaces that had historically been occupied by whites, faced the formidable task of navigating a space that was many times hostile and unwelcoming. Additionally, for the limited numbers of African American students who were enrolled in predominantly white institutions (PWI) of higher education, the experience of being treated as the "other" or as a non-entity by their academic peers, were all too familiar. Yet, conversely, with the formation of HBGLOs, African American students had stable connections to organizations that served to provide safe havens in terms of refuge from hostile institutional climates experienced on campus. As well, students now had common ground in which they could foster meaningful relationships with their African American peers. . . .

Enriching Lives

The students' college lives and experiences and the lives of those they serve were enriched by HBGLOs. The Historically Black Greek Letter Organizations (HBGLOs), often referred to as *The Divine Nine*, include five fraternities (Alpha Phi Alpha, Phi Beta Sigma, Kappa Alpha Psi, Omega Psi Phi, Iota Phi Theta) and four sororities (Alpha Kappa Alpha, Delta Sigma Theta, Sigma Gamma Rho, Zeta Phi Beta). These fraternities and sororities helped students find their place in a hostile climate and make a way for continued success.

Periodical Bibliography

The following articles have been selected to supplement the diverse views presented in this chapter.

Marti Attoun — "House Moms on Campus: Maternal Mentors Feed and Foster College Students," *American Profile*, August 20, 2009.

Samantha Harris — "Stepping into Controversy: Some Fraternity Members Fear Film *Stomp the Yard* Portrays Them as Glamorized Dance Group, Trivializes Traditions," IndependentMail.com (Anderson, SC), January 25, 2007. www.independentmail.com.

Kevin Kittredge — "Parties Pushed Off Campus," *Roanoke Times* (Virginia), October 25, 2009.

Jay Reeves — "Christian Fraternities Offer Different Path," *USA Today*, November 7, 2008.

Jay Reeves — "'Old South' Frat Targeted over Confederate Event," Associated Press, May 13, 2009.

Ronald E. Severtis and C. Andre Christie-Mitzell — "Greek-Letter Membership and College Graduation: Does Race Matter?" *Journal of Sociology and Social Welfare*, September 2007.

Jennifer Sicking — "ISU Grad Studies Impact of Black Sororities," *Tribune Star* (Terre Haute, IN), May 12, 2009.

Michelle Stacey — "My Sorority Dumped Me," *Cosmopolitan*, June 2007.

Brett Wells and Daniel P. Corts — "Measuring Attitudes Towards Sorority and Fraternity Members: Indication of Implicit, Ingroup Favoritism," *College Student Journal*, September 2008.

Nick Wilson — "Cal Poly Changes Its Fraternity Rush Policy After Carson Starkey's Death," *The Tribune* (San Luis Obispo, CA), February 18, 2010.

For Further Discussion

Chapter 1

1. George W. Dowdall warns citizens and policy makers that college drinking is a social problem requiring many resources to solve; Erin M. English, Michael D. Shutt, and Sara B. Oswalt argue that drinking rates are on the decline because of personality differences in the younger generation. How much effort, then, should be put toward changing the culture of college drinking? Is it worth making a significant investment if the next generation of college students does not seem likely to drink habitually? What are the risks of doing nothing?

2. Yale student-journalist Emily Foxhall describes her classmates as a group of people who enjoy frequent sexual gratification without emotional connections, and she reports in the campus newspaper that "hooking up" is common. Jennie Yabroff reassures parents of college students that "hooking up" happens occasionally, but not as often as they might fear. How might the age and audience of the authors affect how the hookup culture is presented and explained?

3. Megan Twohey describes Adderall as a dangerous substance being used by students who are unaware of the risks, while Anne McIlroy argues that it is as beneficial to education as rest and good nutrition. Is there a place in college for a drug that is both harmful and helpful? Are students under academic pressure capable of balancing potential health risks against academic gains? Should other "study drugs" (like caffeine) be similarly regulated? Explain your reasoning.

Chapter 2

1. PRNewswire sites a report that university students may not have adequate access to information about safe sex, but Caitlin Myers suggests that religious schools should not have to be so forthright if the religion frowns on premarital sex among students. Do all university health centers have the same obligation to inform students about the risks of behavior considered by many people to be "immoral"? Do sexual health information and birth control resources undermine a religious school's official philosophy, or do medical care and public health trump moral concerns?

2. John E. Dicken is an optimist about the level of health insurance among college students; Arelis Hernandez is a pessimist about gaps in coverage and the effect of medical problems on academic achievement. Is health insurance coverage a problem that university offices should focus more attention on, or is health care a government's responsibility? If universities spent more resources on meeting students' health needs, would they be able to meet students' academic needs completely? How far into students' personal lives should colleges try to reach?

3. Michael Bogdanoff explains how the nuances of balancing a student's privacy with mental health care can put a university in a precarious legal position. Should a university have more rights to intervene and communicate with a student's parents or guardians, even if a student is a legal adult? Should an individual's privacy be a consideration at all if a school believes that roommates, classmates, or professors are in danger—even slightly—of being harmed?

Chapter 3

1. Rob Jenkins makes the case for competitive athletics programs drawing prospective students and business and local interests to community colleges; Matthew Denhart,

Robert Villwock, and Richard Vedder claim that competitive athletics programs only detract from a university's ability to provide an education. Are these two viewpoints contradictory? Does the size of a school or an athletic department determine if a competitive athletics program is beneficial or detrimental to students? Would informal, intramural sports programs have the same effect?

2. Gary Alan Fine lauds private hazing rituals as important practices that forge important bonds within a team; Jennifer J. Waldron argues that hazing rituals actually create rifts among teammates, no matter how they perceive the experience. Who is the best judge of the effects of hazing rituals? Are student-athletes better able than coaches and school administrators to determine whether hazing improves relationships within their teams?

3. Cathryn L. Claussen interprets the moderate gains in sports opportunity and funding for girls and women at schools over the past thirty-five years as proof that Title IX legislation was necessary and effective. Allison Kasic and Kimberly Schuld believe that the fact that girls and women are not participating in equal numbers after thirty-five years of Title IX support proves that it was unnecessary in the first place. Is thirty-five years enough time to generate interest in sports programs and establish equity between men's and women's athletics? Does Title IX hurt or benefit college athletics? Can equality in sports be legislated?

Chapter 4

1. Sarah Gwin presents the stories of fraternity and sorority members who have had a very positive experience within the Greek system. Is Gwin asking only superficial questions about the Greek experience? Is Gwin's collection of personal anecdotes an accurate guide to understanding what it is like to belong to a fraternity or sorority?

2. Ashlei N. Stevens reports on research that finds members of fraternities and sororities are more likely to binge drink and engage in other risky behaviors than college students not in the Greek system. Sarah Ball criticizes the popular media for always portraying sorority members and other participants in Greek life as shallow and destructive instead of as service oriented and community minded. Are these two characterizations of Greek members mutually exclusive? How likely is it that fraternities and sororities care equally about partying and about developing relationships and performing philanthropy?

3. Black Greek letter organizations (BGLOs) weren't formed until the twentieth century, decades after the mainstream fraternities and sororities were established. Is the relative newness of BGLOs what makes them seem more in tune to current social issues and desires?

Organizations to Contact

The editors have compiled the following list of organizations concerned with the issues presented in this book. The descriptions are derived from materials provided by the organizations. All have publications or information available for interested readers. The list was compiled on the date of publication of the present volume; the information provided here may change. Be aware that many organizations take several weeks or longer to respond to inquiries, so allow as much time as possible.

American College Health Association (ACHA)
891 Elkridge Landing Road, Suite 100, Linthicum, MD 21090
(410) 859-1500 • fax: (410) 859-1510
e-mail: contact@acha.org
Web site: www.acha.org

The American College Health Association (ACHA) is dedicated to the health needs of students at colleges and universities. It is the principal leadership organization for the field of college health and provides services, communications, and advocacy that help its members to advance the health of their campus communities. ACHA publishes the *Journal of College Health*; brochures for students; research white papers; and the quarterly newsletter, *College Health in Action*.

Associated Collegiate Press (ACP)
2221 University Avenue SE, Suite 121,
Minneapolis, MN 55414
(612) 625-8335 • fax: (612) 626-0720
Web site: www.studentpress.org/acp

A division of the National Scholastic Press Association (NSPA), the Associated Collegiate Press (ACP) provides journalism education programs, training materials, media critique and recognition programs, and a forum for members to share and comment on their work. The ACP is the oldest and largest national membership organization for college and university student journalists. It sponsors the Pacemaker Competition and provides awards for reporting, writing, design, photography, and cartooning. It hosts national conventions during the school year and runs summer journalism workshops.

Association for Non-Traditional Students in Higher Education (ANTSHE)

(360) 545-3593 • fax: (866) 887-9940
e-mail: info@antshe.org
Web site: www.antshe.org

The Association for Non-Traditional Students in Higher Education (ANTSHE) is an international partnership of students, academic professionals, institutions, and organizations whose mission is to encourage and coordinate support, education, and advocacy for the non-traditional student—usually a person attending college or university who is older than age twenty-three or who is working full-time, has children, or has other obligations in addition to school. ANTSHE's members are students, professors, and business and community members. The organization publishes the quarterly journal, *The Non-Trad*; sponsors an annual conference; and funds scholarships for graduate and undergraduate students.

BACCHUS Network

PO Box 100430, Denver, CO   80250-0430
(303) 871-0901 • fax: (303) 871-0907
e-mail: admin@bacchusnetwork.org
Web site: www.bacchusgamma.org

The BACCHUS Network is a nonprofit campus and community organization that actively promotes student and young adult leadership on healthy and safe lifestyle decisions concerning alcohol abuse, tobacco use, illegal drug use, unhealthy sexual practices, and other high-risk behaviors. Its philosophy is that students can play a uniquely effective role—unmatched by professional educators—in encouraging their peers to consider, talk honestly about, and develop responsible habits and attitudes toward high-risk health and safety issues. The network produces a training curriculum, manuals, posters, and pamphlets and publishes *Peer Educator* magazine.

Center for the Study of the College Fraternity (CSCF)

900 East Seventh Street, Suite 371, Bloomington, IN   47405
(812) 855-1228
e-mail: cscf@indiana.edu
Web site: www.indiana.edu/~cscf

The Center for the Study of the College Fraternity (CSCF) encourages and supports research on the role of the American college fraternity in higher education. CSCF fulfills this mission in part through research grants, publication of monographs, and the indexing and collection of completed research projects. It is partnered with the Association of Fraternity/Sorority Advisors, which publishes the scholarly journal *Oracle*. CSCF serves mostly as a clearinghouse of information rather than a sponsor of original research; however, it does conduct the Greek Student Experience Survey and the Fraternity and Sorority Experience Survey.

Collegiate Entrepreneurs' Organization (CEO)

815 West Van Buren Street, Suite 400 (MC 244),
Chicago, IL   60607
(773) 360-8426
e-mail: ceo@c-e-o.org
Web site: www.c-e-o.org

The mission of the Collegiate Entrepreneurs' Organization (CEO) is to inform, support, and inspire college students to be entrepreneurial and seek opportunity through enterprise creation. CEO provides student entrepreneurs with opportunities, events, chapter activities, and conferences to help start businesses. It hosts national and regional conferences for students and faculty interested in collegiate entrepreneurship, sponsors student entrepreneur competitions, and runs an online social networking community for members. There are chapters at more than four hundred colleges and universities.

Interfaith Youth Core (IFYC)

910 West Van Buren Street, 4th Floor, Chicago, IL   60607
(312) 573-8825 • fax: (312) 573-1542
e-mail: info@ifyc.org
Web site: www.ifyc.org

Interfaith Youth Core (IFYC) aims to build mutual respect and pluralism among young people from different religious traditions by empowering them to work together to serve others. Its programs include public advocacy to promote the idea of religious pluralism, outreach and education on college campuses and in their communities, and teaching leadership schools to ensure the continuation of the movement. IFYC also provides materials for campus groups wishing to host programs and speakers for events.

National Association of College and University Residence Halls Inc. (NACURH)

726 Broadway, Room 747B, New York, NY   10003
(718) 878-7509
Web site: www.nacurh.org

The National Association of College and University Residence Halls Inc. (NACURH) is considered to be the largest completely student-run organization in the world. NACURH promotes living on campus as an integral part of the college experience and strives to provide resources to help member schools create the ultimate residence hall environment and experience. NACURH provides member resources and hosts an annual conference for students who live in residence halls on college campuses so they can share ideas, resources, and best practices to improve their residential communities.

National Collegiate Athletic Association (NCAA)

700 West Washington Street, PO Box 6222,
Indianapolis, IN   46206-6222
(317) 917-6222 • fax: (317) 917-6888
Web site: www.ncaa.org

The National Collegiate Athletic Association (NCAA) is a voluntary organization through which the nation's colleges and universities govern their athletic programs. It consists of institutions, conferences, organizations, and individuals committed to the education and athletic participation of student-athletes. Its stated purpose is to govern competition in a fair, safe, equitable, and sportsmanlike manner, and to integrate intercollegiate athletics into higher education so that the educational experience of the student-athlete is paramount. It maintains an online library of research, publications, and statistics about sports and NCAA teams and publishes the quarterly magazine *NCAA Champion.*

National Intramural-Recreational Sports Association (NIRSA)

4185 Southwest Research Way, Corvallis, OR   97333-1067
(541) 766-8211 • fax: (541) 766-8284
e-mail: nirsa@nirsa.org
Web site: www.nirsa.org

Serving an estimated 5.5 million students who regularly participate in campus recreational sports programs, National Intramural-Recreational Sports Association (NIRSA) members are actively engaged in many areas of campus life: student leadership, development, and personnel management; wellness and fitness programs; intramural sports; sport clubs; recreation facility operations; outdoor recreation; informal recreation; and aquatic programs. NIRSA publishes *Recreational Sports Journal* and hosts an annual conference and expo.

National Panhellenic Conference (NPC)

3901 West Eighty-sixth Street, Suite 398,
Indianapolis, IN   46268
(317) 872-3185 • fax: (317) 872-3192
e-mail: npccentral@npcwomen.org
Web site: www.npcwomen.org

The National Panhellenic Conference (NPC) provides support and guidance for twenty-six international sororities and women's fraternities and serves as the national voice on contemporary issues of sorority life. It accepts proposals for research about sororities and student life, and it is particularly interested in the topics of parents' perception of sororities and fraternities, attrition and retention rates of members, long-term benefits of membership, alcohol-related behaviors among fraternities and sororities, and the value of mentors within fraternities and sororities. The NPC publishes the free electronic newsletter *Sorority Life*.

One in Four

PO Box 1322, New London, CT   06320
(860) 439-2828 • fax: (860) 439-2897
Web site: www.oneinfourusa.org

One in Four is a national organization dedicated to preventing rape by the thoughtful application of theory and research to rape prevention programming; there are chapters at more than forty colleges and universities. One in Four provides presentations, training, and technical assistance to men and women, with a focus on all-male programming targeted toward colleges, high schools, the military, and local community organizations. The "Men's Program" and the "Women's Program" teach all-male and all-female groups about rape, rape myths, how to recognize potential perpetrators, how to avoid sexually coercive behavior, and how to sympathize with and help victims.

Standing Committee for Lesbian, Gay, Bisexual, and Transgender Awareness (SCLGBTA)

National Center for Higher Education, One Dupont Circle NW, Suite 300, Washington, DC   20036
(202) 835-2272 • fax: (202) 296-3286
e-mail: sclgbta@gmail.com
Web site: www.myacpa.org

The Standing Committee for Lesbian, Gay, Bisexual, and Transgender Awareness (SCLGBTA) is a division of the American College Personnel Association (ACPA). It is dedicated to increasing awareness of the social, psychological, health, and economic realities of lesbian, gay, bisexual, and transgendered people on college campuses. It publishes the newsletter *Out on Campus* and sponsors programs on homosexual and bisexual topics at the annual ACPA convention. The SCLGBTA Web site serves as a resource for information about topics affecting the mental and physical well-being of the community.

Title IX.info
The MARGARET Fund, National Women's Law Center, 11 Dupont Circle NW, Suite 800, Washington, DC   20036
(202) 588-5180
Web site: www.titleix.info

TitleIX.info is a Web site hosted by the National Women's Law Center, under the direction of the May All Resolve, Girls Achieve Real Equity Today (MARGARET) Fund. The site is a resource for people looking for information about all aspects of Title IX—which addresses equality from sports to the sciences and career education—but contains pages specifically about girls' participation in athletic programs. The Web site features profiles of girls and women who have personally benefited from Title IX legislation as well as suggestions for ways visitors can get involved promoting and supporting Title IX, and it also offers visitors information about seeking help if they have experienced problems with violations of Title IX policies.

Bibliography of Books

Kathleen A. Bogle   *Hooking Up: Sex, Dating, and Relationships on Campus.* New York: New York University Press, 2008.

Lane Demas   *Integrating the Gridiron: Black Civil Rights and American College Football.* New Brunswick, NJ: Rutgers University Press, 2010.

Alan D. DeSantis   *Inside Greek U.: Fraternities, Sororities, and the Pursuit of Pleasure, Power, and Prestige.* Lexington, KY: The University Press of Kentucky, 2007.

Ronald G. Ehrenberg, ed.   *What's Happening to Public Higher Education?* Westport, CT: Praeger Publishers, 2006.

Bruce Feldman   *Meat Market: Inside the Smash-Mouth World of College Football Recruiting.* New York: ESPN Books, 2007.

Bonnie S. Fisher, Leah E. Daigle, and Francis T. Cullen   *Unsafe in the Ivory Tower: The Sexual Victimization of College Women.* Los Angeles, CA: Sage Publications, 2010.

Donna Freitas   *Sex and the Soul: Juggling Sexuality, Spirituality, Romance, and Religion on America's College Campuses.* New York: Oxford University Press, 2008.

Andrew Garrod and Robert Kilkenny, eds.

Balancing Two Worlds: Asian American College Students Tell Their Life Stories. Ithaca, NY: Cornell University Press, 2007.

Andrew Garrod, Robert Kilkenny, and Christina Gómez, eds.

Mi Voz, Mi Vida: Latino College Students Tell Their Life Stories. Ithaca, NY: Cornell University Press, 2007.

Richard D. Kadison and Theresa Foy DeGeronimo

College of the Overwhelmed: The Campus Mental Health Crisis and What to Do About It. San Francisco, CA: Jossey-Bass, 2005.

Anya Kamenetz

DIY U: Edupunks, Edupreneurs, and the Coming Transformation of Higher Education. White River Junction, VT: Chelsea Green Publishing, 2010.

David Leibow

What to Do when College Is Not the Best Time of Your Life. New York: Columbia University Press, 2010.

Leslie Miller-Bernal and Susan L. Poulson

Going Coed: Women's Experiences in Formerly Men's Colleges and Universities, 1950–2000. Nashville, TN: Vanderbilt University Press, 2004.

A. Rafik Mohamed & Erik D. Fritsvold

Dorm Room Dealers: Drugs and the Privileges of Race and Class. Boulder, CO: Lynne Rienner Publishers, 2010.

Michele A. Paludi, ed.

Understanding and Preventing Campus Violence. Westport, CT: Praeger Publishers, 2008.

Randal Pinkett — *Campus CEO: The Student Entrepreneur's Guide to Launching a Multimillion-Dollar Business.* Chicago, IL: Kaplan Publishing, 2007.

Sheila Riddell, Teresa Tinklin, and Alastair Wilson — *Disabled Students in Higher Education: Perspectives on Widening Access and Changing Policy.* New York: Routledge, 2005.

Kevin Roose — *The Unlikely Disciple: A Sinner's Semester at America's Holiest University.* New York: Grand Central Publishing, 2009.

Michael L. Siegel — *Race to Injustice: Lessons Learned from the Duke Lacrosse Rape Case.* Durham, NC: Carolina Academic Press, 2009.

Cynthia G. Simpson and Vicky G. Spencer — *College Success for Students with Learning Disabilities: Strategies and Tips to Make the Most of Your College Experience.* Waco, TX: Prufrock Press, 2009.

Laura Sessions Stepp — *Unhooked: How Young Women Pursue Sex, Delay Love and Lose at Both.* New York: Riverhead Books, 2007.

Burton A. Weisbrod, Jeffrey P. Ballou, and Evelyn D. Asch — *Mission and Money: Understanding the University.* New York: Cambridge University Press, 2008.

Shane L. Windmeyer, ed. — *Brotherhood: Gay Life in College Fraternities.* New York: Alyson Books, 2005.

Mark Yost

Varsity Green: A Behind the Scenes Look at Culture and Corruption in College Athletics. Stanford, CA: Stanford University Press, 2010.

Index

H

H Bomb (magazine), 49, 51

Harvard University
drinking patterns studies, 22, 23–24
student sexual behavior, 43, 49–52

Hazing
dangerous and harmful, 128–134
defined, 129
high schools, 130
incidence, 132
legal issues, 131
strengthens teams, 124–127

HBGLOs. *See* Historically black Greek letter organizations (HBGLOs)

Health care
campus offices and services, 78, 79, 90, 93, 96, 177
doctors' over-prescribing, 55–56, 57
mental health services, 103
students should take responsibility for sexual health, 76–83
uninsured students, 85–86, 87, 92, 93, 94–95, 96–97
universities need to provide better sexual health services, 69–75, 78

Health insurance
colleges' student plans, 85, 86–88, 89–90, 95
enrollment prerequisite, 87–88, 90, 95
most students have adequate insurance, 84–91
students are underinsured, 92–97

Health Insurance Portability and Accountability Act (HIPAA) (1996), 90–91, 102

Heiligenstein, Eric, 56

Hendler, Stewart, 179

Hernandez, Arelis, 92–97

High school athletics, 140, 141–142

Hingson, Ralph, 25, 27, 29–30

HIPAA (Health Insurance Portability and Accountability Act) (1996), 90–91, 102

Historically black Greek letter organizations (HBGLOs), 182, 184–186

H1N1, 66–67

Hockey programs, 117

"Hookup" culture
is exaggerated by the media, 48–52
is widespread, 41–47

The House Bunny (film), 180

Housing. *See* Dormitories; Eviction and expelling; Housing codes and suicide; Sorority housing

Housing codes and suicide, 99–100, 101, 103–104

Howard University, 182

Human papillomavirus, 82

Hunter College, 99–100

I

Illegal drugs. *See* Drug abuse

Immunization
legal issues, 67–68
meningitis, 66, 67

In loco parentis, 14, 15, 102–103, 104